WATERCOLOUR
by Charlotte, Viscountess Canning
Lady in Waiting to Queen Victoria

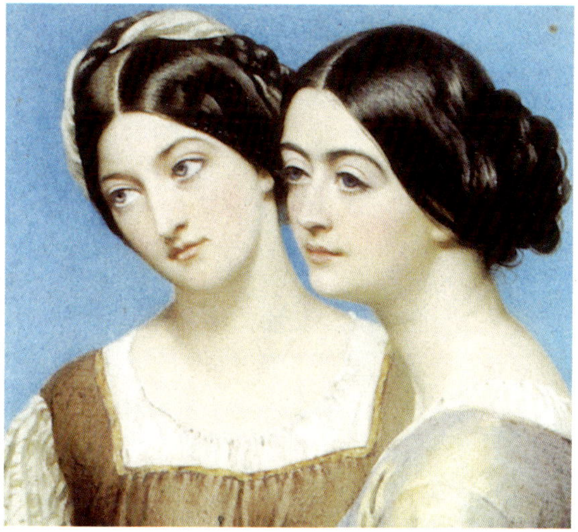

Delia Millar

HAREWOOD

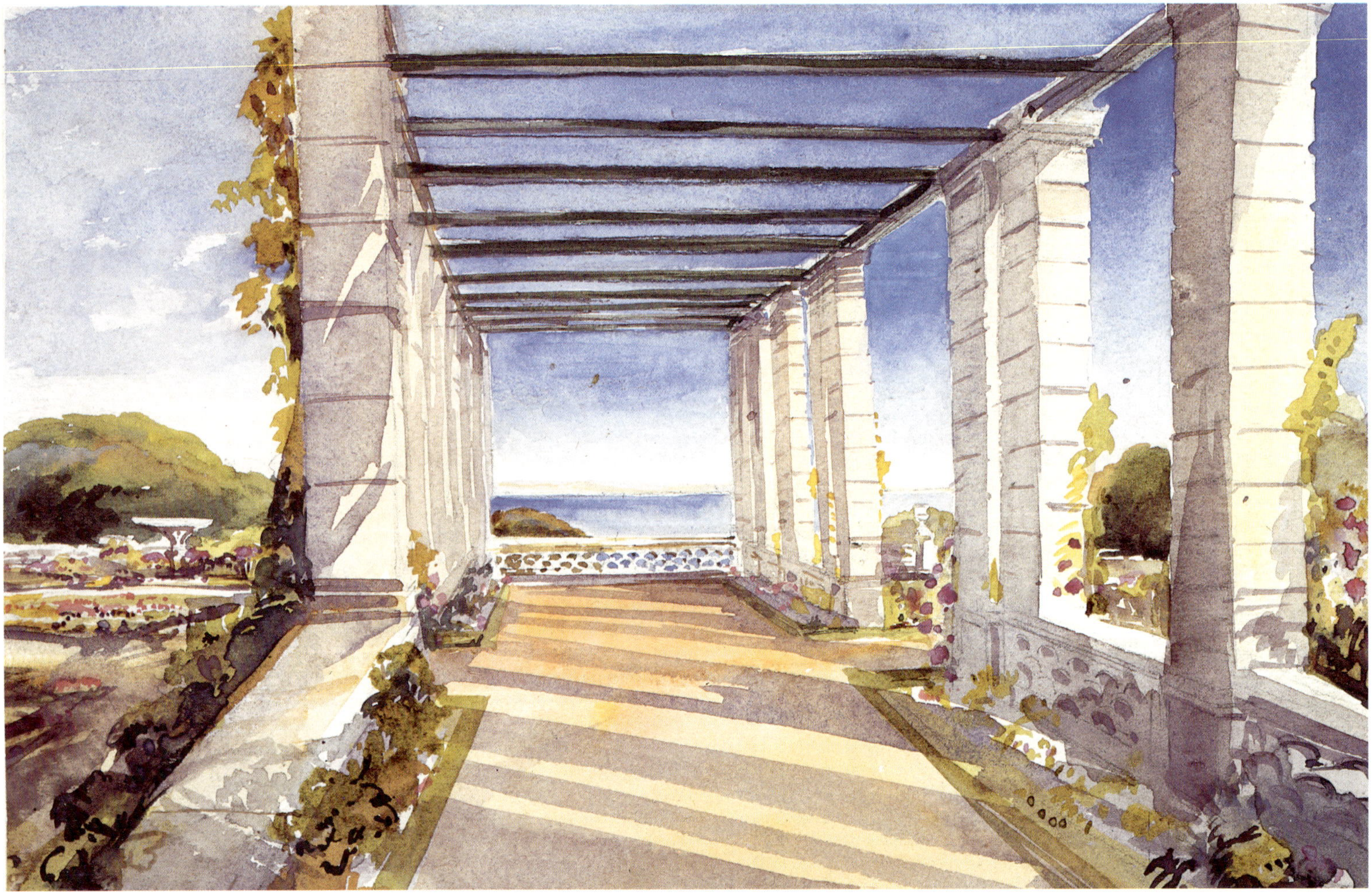

Osborne House – the Vinery (see page 30).

Foreword by Lord Harewood

The watercolours by Lady Canning have not, unlike those of her sister, Louisa, Marchioness of Waterford, been exhibited in public before. They have remained hidden – unexplored treasure – inside large volumes in the Library at Harewood House. Three were shown at the exhibition of 'Harewood Masterpieces – English Watercolours and Drawings' at Christie's, King Street, London, in January 1996, where, even surrounded by work by J.M.W. Turner and Thomas Girtin, they stood up well.

Neither Lady Canning nor her sister, Lady Waterford, had children. After her husband's death in 1862 Lady Canning's watercolours and drawings, her photographs and her journals passed to Lord Canning's nephew, Lord Hubert de Burgh (later Lord Clanricarde). Apart from three watercolours which were apparently framed by Lady Canning to be sent to exhibitions, the rest of the watercolours are mounted in large volumes, the earlier ones by Lady Canning herself. The others were bound up by my father, to whom Lady Canning's possessions passed by descent. One volume, bound in brown leather with two metal clasps, with the date 1839-40 on the spine, survives and was obviously made up for Lady Canning herself. Of the further volumes there are twelve bound in green leather and cloth, by the London binder Morrell, which contain her landscape watercolours. In these all the inscriptions which date from before her journey to India are in Lady Canning's hand. Three large red leather volumes contain watercolours of flowers and other plants. A few were painted before Lady Canning went to India in 1856, but the majority are large watercolours of exotic Indian plants painted out there. Many of these watercolours were sent home to her mother to avoid damage from the Indian climate. Lady Canning never returned to England to see them again.

When before the War my brother and I were at Harewood on holiday from school, we used occasionally to look over my father's shoulder at the drawings – mainly Italian – he had collected throughout his life. These were kept in great portfolios and put on a card table. I am not quite certain at what age this changed from a chore to a treat but we were also introduced to one of the volumes of Lady Canning's drawings. These were taken out from time to time and we listened to a description of what they were and where they were painted. They varied considerably, some mere sketches for pictures which had gone to Queen Victoria, others a finished product. And they covered everything visual that had caught her attention – views, flowers, places abroad, aspects of India – so that in effect the volumes of collected drawings were like a vast photograph album.

My brother and I probably learnt a little about geography (not otherwise a popular school subject) from Lady Canning's drawings, but I think we also started an element of appreciation of art. I have never tired of looking at them – perhaps not surprising since at Harewood there are a lot to choose from.

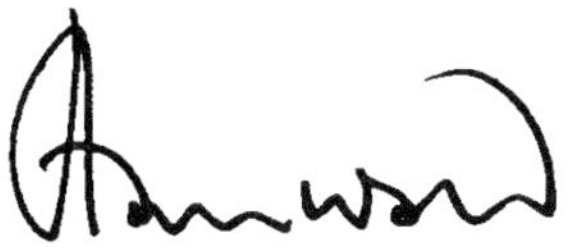

Introduction

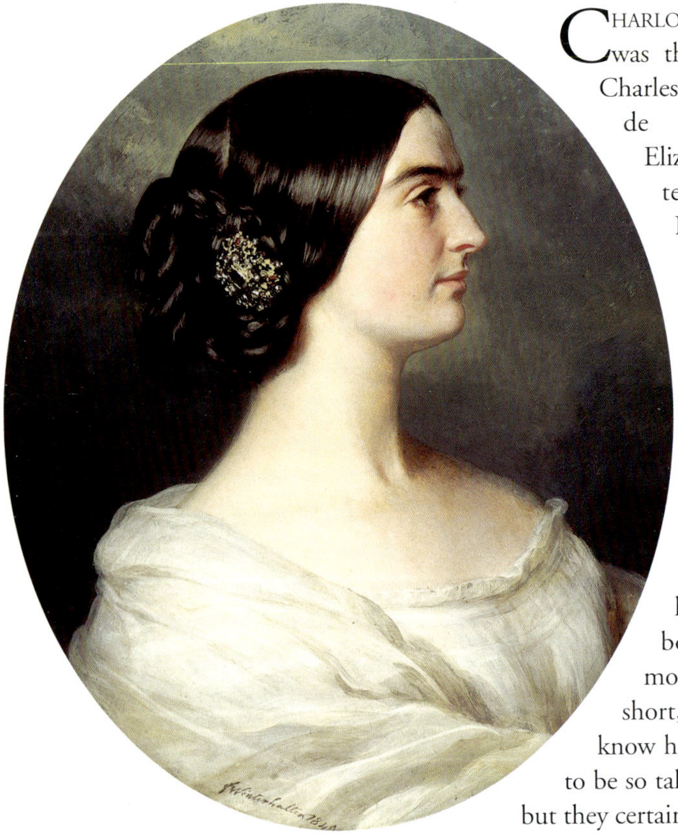

Franz Winterhalter: Charlotte, Viscountess Canning *(see page 8).*

CHARLOTTE STUART (1817-1861) was the elder daughter of Sir Charles Stuart (later Lord Stuart de Rothesay) and Lady Elizabeth Yorke, third daughter of the 3rd Earl of Hardwicke. She and her sister, Louisa, were partly brought up in Paris, where their father was British Ambassador from 1815 to 1830, and they travelled on the Continent. The girls were 'supposed to be the most lovely sisters of that time, though I have always heard that both their father and mother were extremely plain, short, and stumpy, so I don't know how the two girls managed to be so tall, graceful and handsome, but they certainly were, and very talented as well'(1). Both daughters were enthusiastic artists: G.F. Watts later said of Louisa the younger sister that she 'believed she was *born* an artist greater than any England has produced, the circumstances of her life alone preventing her from working on to the full achievement'. The artist William Simpson was to describe Louisa as a 'real artist', whereas her sister 'would rank as a very clever amateur'(2).

Louisa married the 3rd Marquis of Waterford in 1842. In her painting, again almost all in watercolour, she concentrated on figure and subject pictures, whereas the elder sister painted almost entirely landscapes, and had lessons from J.D. Harding and William Leitch.

Charlotte married Charles Canning in 1835, and he succeeded his mother as 2nd Viscount Canning in 1837. 'In marrying Charlotte Stuart he knew he had secured one of the accepted beauties of her day, he did not realise at once, nor till much later, almost too late, that hers was a nature of the rarest kind, compact of goodness, joy, peace, love and long-suffering, but so delicately poised that the smallest misunderstanding or neglect might shatter the fabric of her happiness. How he came near doing so belongs to a later date, and was undreamt of when these two knelt together and exchanged vows that were faithfully carried out by Charlotte Elizabeth and intermittently by Charles John'(3). In May 1842 Lady Canning received an invitation from the Queen to become her Lady of the Bedchamber, a post she held until, in 1855, she had to resign to accompany her husband to India as Governor-General, and later Viceroy (he was created Earl Canning in 1859). The Queen added that: 'As I have had the pleasure of knowing you, ever since *we were* Children, I sh^{ld} be very happy if this w^{ld} suit you'(4). She accepted, and was in Waiting for the first time the next month. By 20 December the Queen had decided that Lady Canning was 'a remarkably nice person, so quiet, unaffected & gentle & so ready to do anything' (5).

Lady Canning found the Queen 'very kind pleasant and I do not at all dislike being here'(6).

Lady Canning commanded great respect from her fellow Ladies in Waiting and Maids of Honour. Lady Lyttelton, Governess to the royal children, described how she had had 'a very pleasant talk with Lady Canning... she is exceedingly agreeable and admirable in every way, I think, – so simple and unselfish'(7). Mary Bulteel, who was to marry Henry Ponsonby, Queen Victoria's Private Secretary, in 1861, wrote as a young Maid of Honour in 1854 that going into Waiting was 'the beginning of a fresh lot of experiences' and 'a wider aspect of life'. She found 'the companionship of older & most excellent women such as Lady Jocelyn & Lady Canning very wholesome'. Their kindness and companionship eased her relations with them and others in Waiting. She thought Lady Canning a great influence for good, and while she praised Lady Jocelyn, as having a charm that 'was indefinable – it appeared to me that every body else was so tiresome, ugly, uninteresting & altogether objectionable – No! Lady Canning was an exception I had more of an exalted reverential culte for her, a greater admiration, but Lady Jocelyn amused me, oh *amused* me beyond words' (8).

One of the Queen's requirements for her Ladies in Waiting or her Maids of Honour was that, if possible, they could draw or paint, or could play duets with her and accompany her when she sang to the piano. Lady Canning was the most accomplished of the artists among her Ladies. She painted many watercolours of the places that she saw while on duty during the thirteen years she served as Lady in Waiting. Some places visited by the Queen when Lady Canning was not on duty, she drew for her on other occasions.

The Queen was, of course, an equally enthusiastic amateur artist. The Maid of Honour, Eleanor Stanley, who found Lady Canning 'all that is charming', describes how Lady Canning had to give the Queen 'regular lessons, like a master, and the Queen said, "What shall I put now?" – "Do you think I should add some green?" "Is that blue enough?" – and did exactly as she was bid'(9). Lady Canning, who had been having lessons with William Leitch, introduced him to the Queen. For many years he subsequently taught the Queen and her children to paint landscapes in watercolour. In her work Lady Canning can be seen to be using Leitch's technique of painting in pure watercolour with the addition of white heightening, and occasional use of bodycolour and gum arabic. The buff, cream or blue-grey paper which she habitually uses has not been noted in the entries, nor has the use of pencil which is usually visible under the final watercolour.

Queen Victoria was anxious that, whenever possible, Lady Canning should be on duty when an expedition took place. The rota of Waiting was rearranged so that she would be in attendance during the first voyage on the new royal yacht, the *Victoria and Albert,* along the south and south-west coast, and then across to France in August 1843. On the Queen's visit to Scotland in 1844 Lady Canning drew the environs of Blair Castle for the Queen and in 1845 she illustrated the Queen's first visit to Germany.

There are a number of views of Osborne and of Balmoral and especially of the country round about, up to her last visit there in 1853. If the Queen visited a place at a time when Lady Canning was not on duty, she was often persuaded to give the Queen a watercolour of it made there when on a private visit.

At the time of Lady Canning's arrival at court in 1842 the Queen and Prince Albert were enthusiastically beginning to compile the volumes of watercolours and drawings which became known as the Souvenir or View Albums. These were to consist of nine volumes, compiled in chronological order, containing over 600 images collected during the twenty-one years of their married life and illustrating

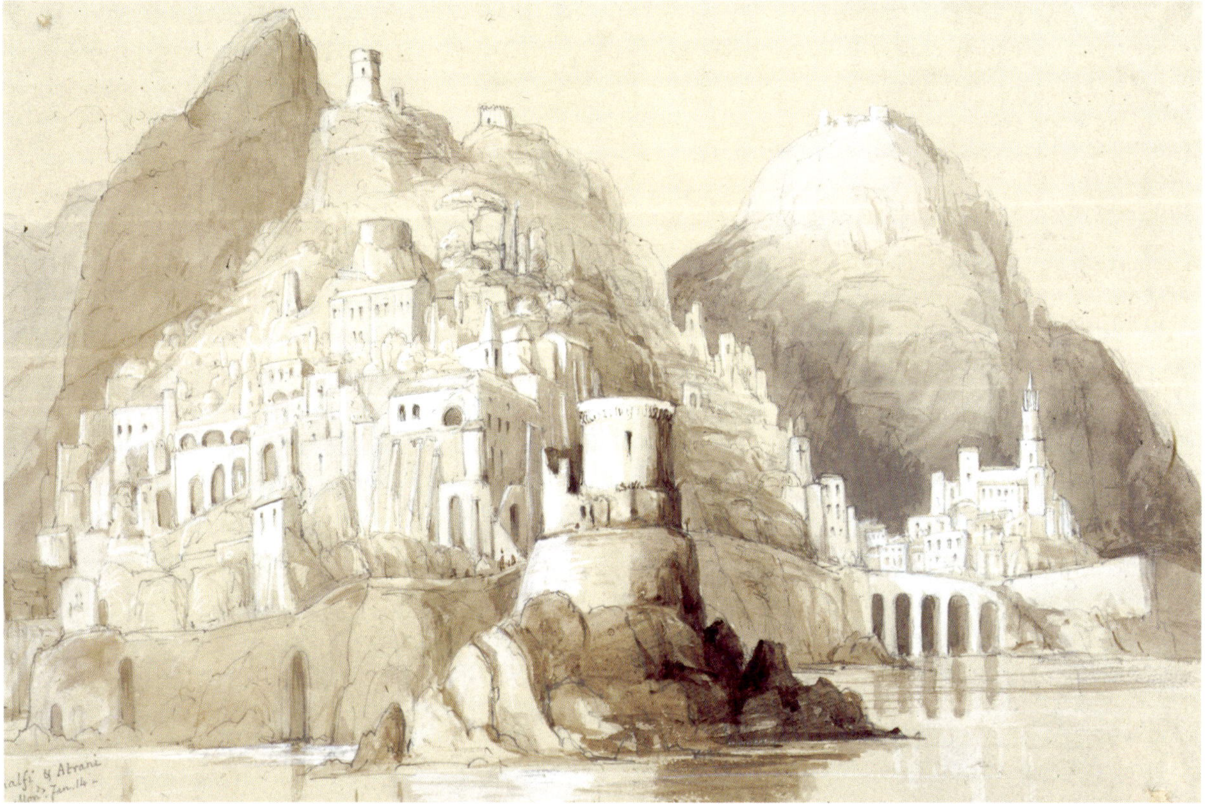

Amalfi and Atrani *(see page 10).*

places they visited and events they had witnessed. Of the seventy watercolours painted by Lady Canning for Queen Victoria the majority were mounted in these Souvenir Albums, beginning with views of that first expedition along the south coast in 1843.

In a number of cases the watercolours and sketches at Harewood House relate to those made by Lady Canning for the Queen. Some, like her sketch on Arran *(page 24),* or the pencil study, inked over, of Schloss Callenberg *(page 17)* are obviously rough studies made on the spot which could be translated at home into more elaborate watercolours. Lady Canning had a sort of love-hate relationship with her work for the Queen. She wrote on board the royal yacht at Cologne: 'I was ordered to draw all day long & there was no use making a fuss about it, 20 or 30 bad little scratches were produced'.

Charlotte Canning was a determined artist. At Welbeck Abbey on 13 November 1843, she told her mother that she had been trying in vain to copy miniatures and large oil paintings in the house and 'I am discouraged to find my drawing powers are limited to bad out of door sketches', though she was prepared to persist as it was best 'to try all sorts of things as every style improves one'(10).

Her talents were certainly developed in her later years with the beautiful flower paintings made in India and the views in that country. She seems to have worked with more freedom in India, without the restraint of working for the Queen's Souvenir Albums. Lady Canning's mother told her that John Ruskin said that her botanical paintings 'were the grandest representations of flowers he had ever seen. He said what a *subtle* use of colours you displayed...'(11).

Lady Canning's death at the early age of forty-four brought to an end the career of this talented and attractive lady, described by Sir Richard Temple as 'the most gifted Englishwoman that had ever landed in India'(12).

NOTES: Abbreviations here, and in the entries, are as follows:

Journal: Queen Victoria's Journal, in the Royal Archives at Windsor Castle.

VS: Virginia Surtees, *Charlotte Canning* (1975).

Canning papers: unpublished letters and travel diaries of Charlotte, Viscountess Canning, in the possession of the Earl of Harewood. Lady Canning wrote especially to her mother and sister, and her travel journals were passed round her family. In quoting from these papers no corrections to her punctuation have been made.

RL and DM: Inventory numbers of watercolours in the Royal Collection.

1. Lady Clodagh Anson, *Victorian Days* (1957), p. 22
2. *The Autobiography of William Simpson R.I,* ed. G.Eyre Todd (1903), p. 104
3. Hon. Mrs Edward (Violet) Stuart-Wortley, *Highcliffe and the Stuarts* (1927), p. 324
4. Canning papers *(see p. 36)*
5. Journal
6. Canning papers
7. *Correspondence of Sarah Spencer, Lady Lyttelton 1787-1870,* ed. Hon Mrs Hugh Wyndham (1912), p. 330
8. Ponsonby papers, Shulbrede Priory
9. *Twenty Years at Court, Memoirs & letters of the Hon. Eleanor Stanley, Maid of Honour, 1842-1862,* ed. Mrs Steuart Erskine (1916), p.95,12: 21 March 1845 and 30 September 1846
10. Canning papers, 14 August 1845, 13 November 1843
11. VS, p. 265
12. Sir R. Temple, Lieutenant-Governor of Bengal, *The Story of my Life* (1896), I, p.76

Acknowledgments
Quotations from Queen Victoria's Journal and other papers in the Royal Archives, Windsor Castle, are made by Gracious Permission of Her Majesty The Queen. References from the Canning diaries and papers are made by kind permission of the Earl of Harewood (the papers are deposited at the Leeds District Archive Service, Sheepscar Library, Leeds). The Ponsonby papers at Shulbrede Priory are quoted by permission of the family. Virginia Surtees, *Charlotte Canning* (1975) has been extensively used and quoted and the author's help and generosity is much appreciated.

For further reading on Lady Canning's work for Queen Victoria see D. Millar, *The Victorian Watercolours and Drawings in the Collection of H.M. the Queen* (1995), and for her time in India see Charles Allen, *A Glimpse of the Burning Plain* (1986).

The Pictures

Portraits

FRANZ XAVER WINTERHALTER (1805-73)
Portrait and genre painter, who pursued a successful career at the courts of Europe and worked extensively for Queen Victoria from 1842.

Charlotte, Viscountess Canning
Canvas, oval. 63.2 x 50.2 cm *(see page 4)*
Signed and dated *f Winterhalter 1849*
Provenance: painted for Queen Victoria; given to the 6th Earl of Harewood by King George V.
Literature: T. Borenius, *Catalogue of the Pictures and Drawings at Harewood House* (1936), no. 102; R. Ormond and C. Blackett-Ord, *Franz Xaver Winterhalter and the Courts of Europe 1830-70,* exhibition National Portrait Gallery, London and Petit Palais, Paris, 1988, no. 35; O. Millar, *The Victorian Pictures in the Collection of H.M. The Queen* (1992), p. 285.

Head and shoulders in profile to right. Painted in 1849 for Queen Victoria, *en suite* with Winterhalter's portraits of her other Ladies in Waiting, Lady Jocelyn and Lady Douro. The Queen wrote on 31 July 1849: 'Winterhalter has sent the 2 heads he has painted for me, of Lady Canning & Fanny Jocelyn, which are extremely like. We...had a visit from good Winterhalter himself, whom we took to the dining-room to see how his pictures looked hung up, and he was much pleased' (Journal).

When, on 16 August 1890, Lady Waterford saw this portrait of her sister on her only visit to Osborne, she thought it 'rather like, but hard' (A.Hare, *The Story of Two Noble Lives* (1893), III, p. 470).

Right: After Franz Winterhalter: Queen Victoria.

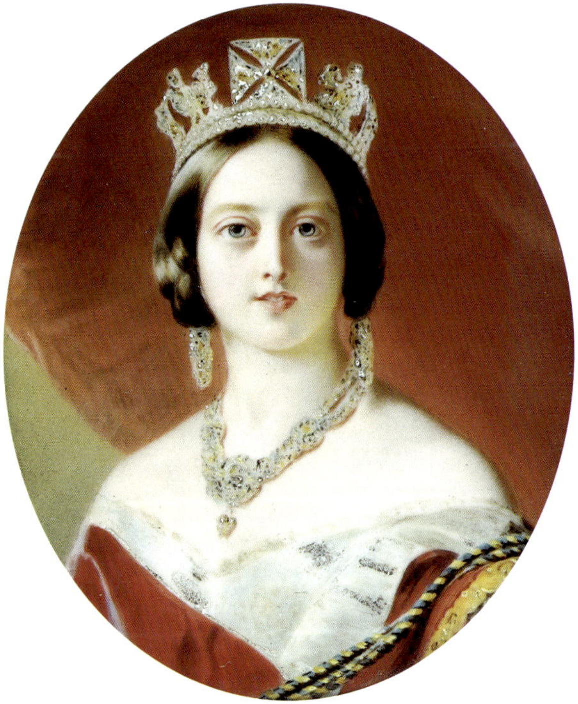

AFTER WINTERHALTER
Queen Victoria (1819-1901)
Ivory, oval 10 x 8.5 cm
Provenance: given to Mary, Princess Royal, Countess of Harewood, by Queen Mary, on 1 January 1937.

Copy in miniature of the head and shoulders from the full-length oil portrait painted by Winterhalter for Queen Victoria in 1843 (see O. Millar, *The Victorian Pictures in the Collection of H.M. The Queen* (1992), no. 811). The Queen wears the circlet, with ear-rings and necklace made from diamonds given to her by the Sultan Mahmúd II of

Turkey in 1838. Of the innumerable miniature copies that exist, versions by Essex, Faija, Moira and Simpson are documented.

ROBERT THORBURN (1818-85)

Miniature painter. Studied at the Scottish Academy and the Royal Academy Schools in London. Exhibited at the Royal Academy, 1837-84.

Charlotte, Viscountess Canning,
and Louisa, Marchioness of Waterford

Panel, circular top. 50.2 x 33.3 cm

Provenance: by descent from Lord Clanricarde.

Literature: Tancred Borenius, *Catalogue of the Pictures and Drawings at Harewood House* (1936), no. 464.

Engraved: Augustus Hare, *The Story of Two Noble Lives,* (1893), frontispiece, vol. I, upper part only.

Two full-length figures on a terrace, with landscape background – Lady Canning is on the right.

A version in watercolour on ivory (50.5 x 34 cm), was purchased in 1949 for the Scottish National Portrait Gallery (PG 1530). A third version at Eastnor Castle, Ledbury, Herefordshire was painted for the sitter's cousin, Charles, 3rd Earl Somers.

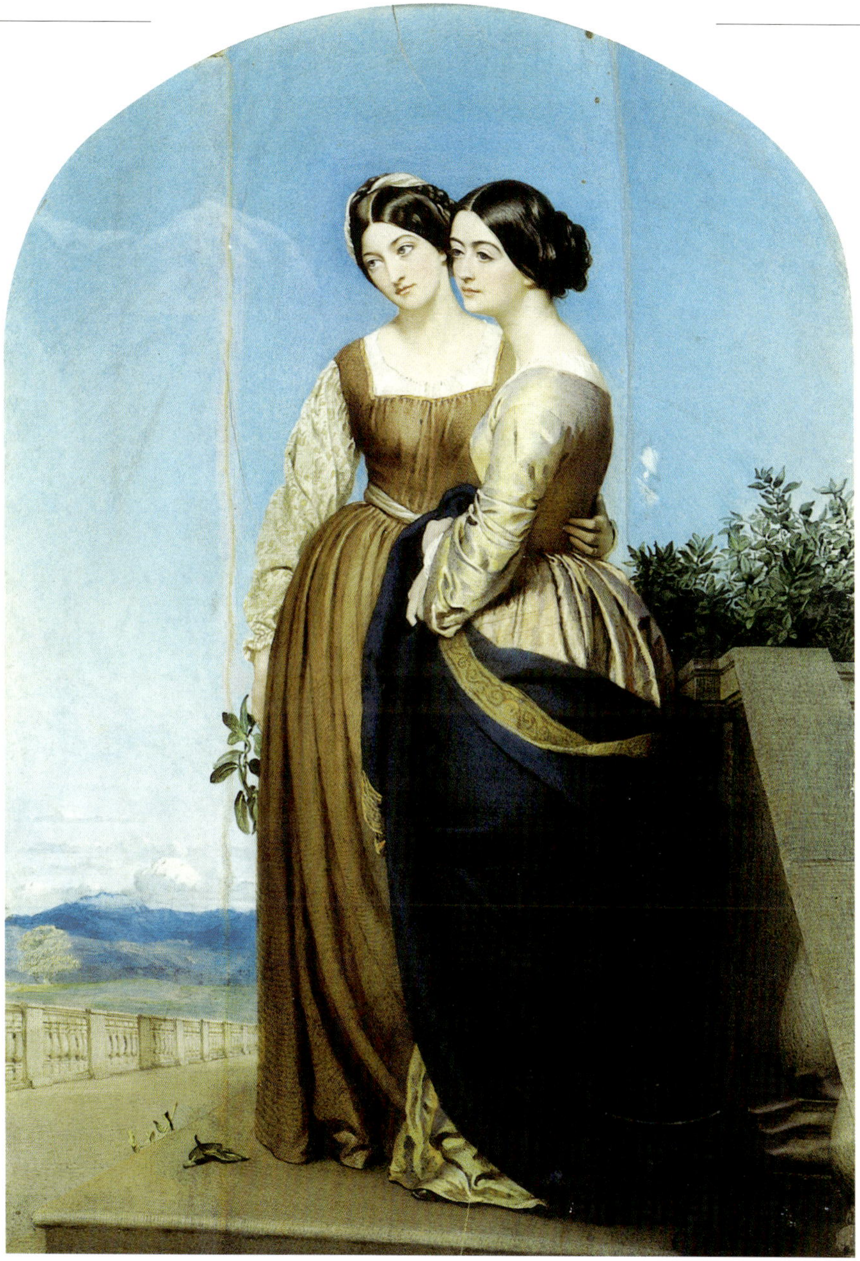

Robert Thorburn: Charlotte, Viscountess Canning and Louisa, Marchioness of Waterford.

Private Travels

FROM HER MARRIAGE IN 1835 Charlotte, Viscountess Canning, travelled extensively with her husband, especially to visit friends in this country and to explore the Continent. Many journeys were made by private yacht, and also by the new railway systems. The Cannings were in Rome in February 1841 and, having travelled from Heidelberg, they spent the winter of 1846-7 in Rome.

Amalfi and Atrani
Sepia ink and wash with white heightening.
25.9 x 36.6 cm *(see page 6)*
Dated and inscribed *Amalfi & Atrani / Mon[dy] Jan. 14.*

Heidelberg (see page 11).

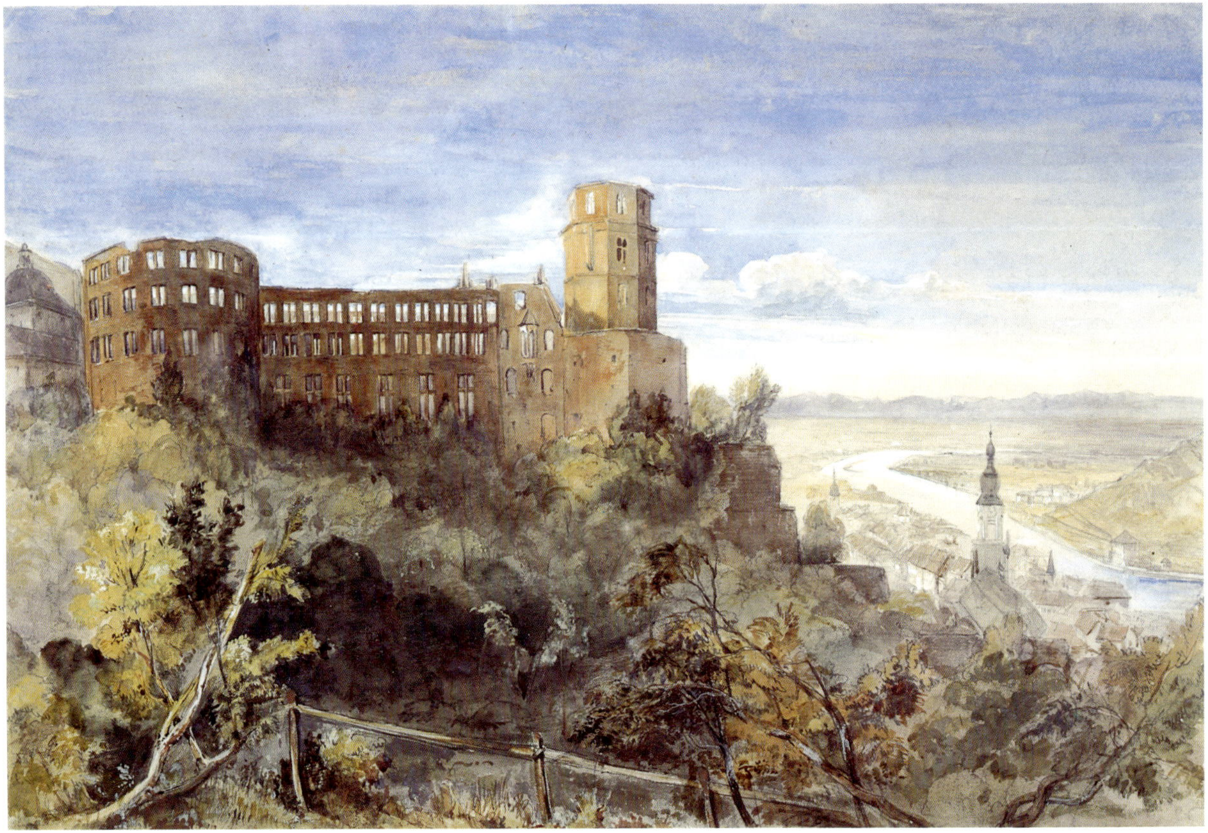

Presumably drawn from the Cannings' yacht moored off the shore. The rocky eminence with the ruins of the Castello Pontone (with the round tower on the summit of the hill) separates the towns of Amalfi and Atrani (on right).

Between August 1838 and April 1839 the Cannings travelled as far as Athens on their new yacht, *Gondola.* The following year they visited Corunna, Gibraltar, Genoa and Palermo, before sailing on to Constantinople.

Heidelberg

Watercolour with white heightening. 31.7 x 47 cm

Signed on mount *C Canning*

Showing the castle of the Electors of the Palatinate, completed in the seventeenth century, but remaining as a splendid ruin after it was largely destroyed by French troops in the 1680s.

On 16 October 1846 the Earl of Malmesbury records leaving Heidelberg by railway with the Cannings whom he had met there. The watercolour may have been painted by Lady Canning on this visit *(Memoirs of an Ex-Minister, Earl of Malmesbury GCB* (1884), I, p.176).

Copy after *Sir Kenelm Digby and his family* by Sir Anthony Van Dyck

Watercolour with gum arabic. 14.6 x 18.2 cm

Inscribed on mount *Sir Endymion Porter & Lady Venetia. Van Dyck at Welbeck*

A copy by Lady Canning from the oil painting then at Welbeck Abbey, and entitled by her *Sir Endymion Porter and Lady Venetia Digby* (see exh. cat., '*Death, Passion and Politics*', Dulwich Picture Gallery 1995-6, no 23).

At Christmas 1836 the Cannings stayed at Welbeck Abbey with the 4th Duke and Duchess of Portland. The Duchess was Lord Canning's maternal aunt. They were at Welbeck again in 1843 when Lady Canning tried, like her sister Louisa, to copy oil paintings in watercolour, but she told her mother that she had tried in vain to copy miniatures in the house, and had tried sketching 'from large oil paintings with very little success' (Canning papers, 13 November 1843). Many small copies of pictures are mounted in the earliest volume of Lady Canning's works, with landscapes, many in sepia, painted in the 1830s. They are much less elaborate and less free than her later works.

British flowers

Nine small watercolours mounted on p. 4 of vol.I of Lady Canning's three volumes of 'Drawings of English & Indian Flowers'. The places where she drew the species are sometimes noted in brackets. They are inscribed, left to right,

Top row:

Vicia Sylvatica: Wood Vetch
SAXIFRAGA AIZOIDES : Yellow Mountain Saxifrage
DROSERA LONGIFOLIA : Sundew
Fumaria Capreolata: Ramping Fumitory (St Mary's Isle)

Middle row:

Sea Buckthorn (Islay)
Geranium Sanguineum (St Mary's Isle)
Rubus Chamaemorus : Cloudberry

Bottom row:

Eri... nigrum: Crimson Li...berry (Dunrobin)
Hybiscum [Hypericum] *Pulchrum: Small upright St John's Wort (Dunrobin)*
Sorbus Saxa... cus: [Rubus Saxatalis or Sylvaticus] *Stone Bramble (Islay, September)*
Polygala vulgaris: [Milkwort]

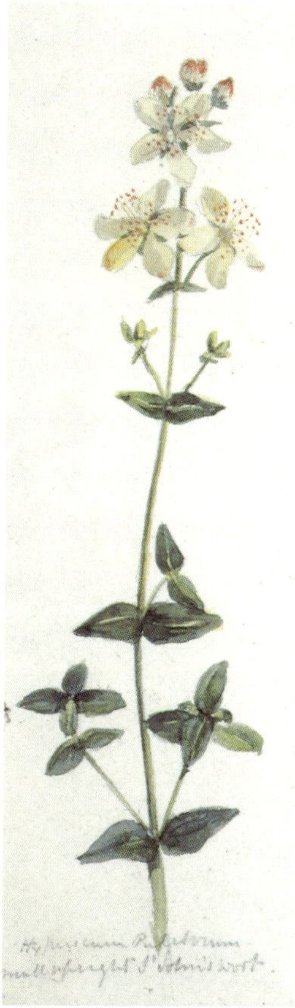

British Flowers – Hybiscum [Hypericum] *Pulchrum.*

Visits to Rome

THE CANNINGS WERE STAYING IN ROME in 1841 when Lady Canning told her mother on 27 February: 'I have seen no end of churches and pictures & studios, but it would be endless to tell you which'. By 16 March she told her that 'we have almost finished the first round of sights which has been hard enough work to make us look forward to another winter at Rome without any duty of seeing sights as a much greater pleasure but I have enjoyed it very much indeed when I was not tired to death and now I like it better and better every day. The weather is bright and fine & not too cold'. The Cannings visited Nemi, Frascati, Tivoli and Ostia before moving on to Siena, Florence and Genoa on their way home.

They returned to Rome in 1846, for a stay of five months, when Charlotte Canning wrote home that she had made 'very few sketches hitherto, but I hope to bring home a full portfolio, for I am more than ever delighted with the beautiful & peculiar scenery of the Campagna. The subjects for drawing & in the villas are quite innumerable' (Canning papers).

In July 1849 Lady Canning stayed with her sister at Curraghmore. Lady Waterford told her mother of Lady Canning's watercolours: 'She has a *magnificent* collection of Italian ones; I think them most masterly, and those coloured on the spot particularly good. Waterford is much interested in them, and says truly – "Loo couldn't do that"...'(A. Hare, *The Story of Two Noble Lives* (1893), I, p.324).

Below: View from a vineyard north of Rome.

Opposite: Cathedral of Santiago de Compostela.

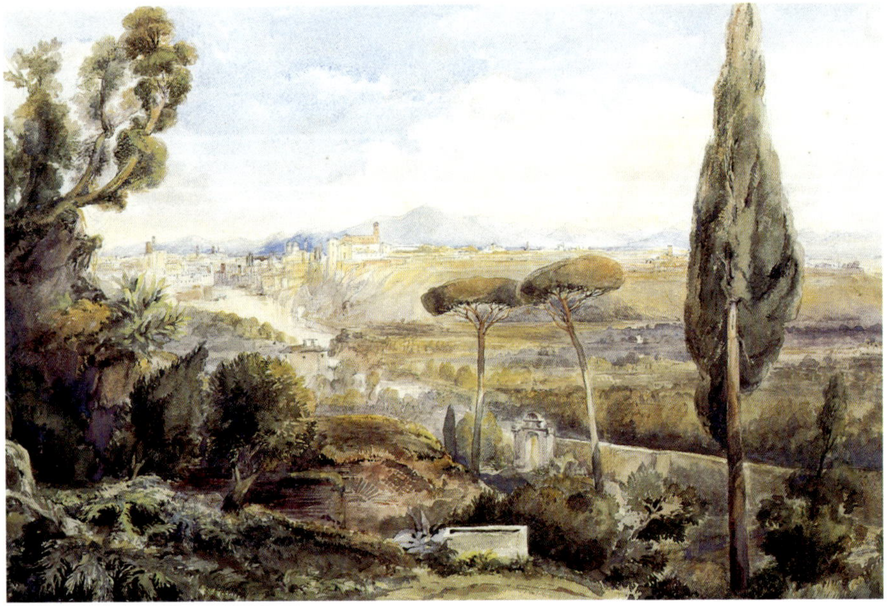

View from a vineyard north of Rome
Watercolour. 35.4 x 51.5 cm
Verso of frame: inscribed by the artist on a label: *Sketch from a vineyard on the North side of Rome / Viscountess Canning / to be returned to 10 Grosvenor Square,* with the digit 2

Probably drawn during the winter of 1846-7 when the Cannings were in Rome. On 8 January she told her mother that 'we have been riding & drawing & sightseeing all very pleasant but not amusing to tell about, the time passes very quickly'. Presumably mounted, framed and sent to a loan exhibition by the artist. A first version, less elaborately finished, of the same size, is in one of Lady Canning's albums.

Palazzo Corsini, Rome, from the gardens
Watercolour, bodycolour and white heightening.
34.2 x 27.2 cm
Inscribed on mount *Corsini Palace.*

A view from the gardens looking down on the palazzo

with, perhaps, the dome of S. Andrea della Valle in the distance. Mounted in Lady Canning's album dated 1846 and presumably drawn during her visit to Rome in the winter of 1846-7, as the leaves are off the trees.

The palace is described by Augustus Hare, with behind it on the slope of Monte Gianicolo, the 'large and beautiful Gardens, adorned with fountains, cypresses, and some grand old plane-trees'. There we are told that Queen Christina, who died in the palace in 1689, presided over the first meetings of the Arcadian Academy (Augustus Hare, *Walks in Rome* (1878), II, pp. 463-9).

Landscape with sheds, silver birch trees beside water and an upturned barrel in centre
Watercolour. 34 x 52 cm
Verso: inscribed on a label as *by the Viscountess Canning / To be returned*

Possibly a landscape in Scotland, with hilly background. Presumably mounted and framed by the artist to be sent to a loan exhibition.

Cathedral of Santiago de Compostela
Watercolour with white heightening. 50.5 x 34.5 cm
Inscribed *Cathedral of Santiago. / (Torre del Reloj) / Aug 3. 1852.*

Described by Baedeker, the universally used guidebook, as the most important monument of the early Romanesque style in Spain. This watercolour shows the twelfth-century south front of the transept, the Puerta de Platerias, with, on the right, the 262 ft Torre de la Trinidad (of which the upper part dates from 1680).

In July 1852, Lady Canning joined her new yacht, the *Fair Rosamund*, at Cowes when she came off duty at Osborne *(see page 36)*. The Cannings sailed from Plymouth to Vigo and from there travelled overland to reach Santiago

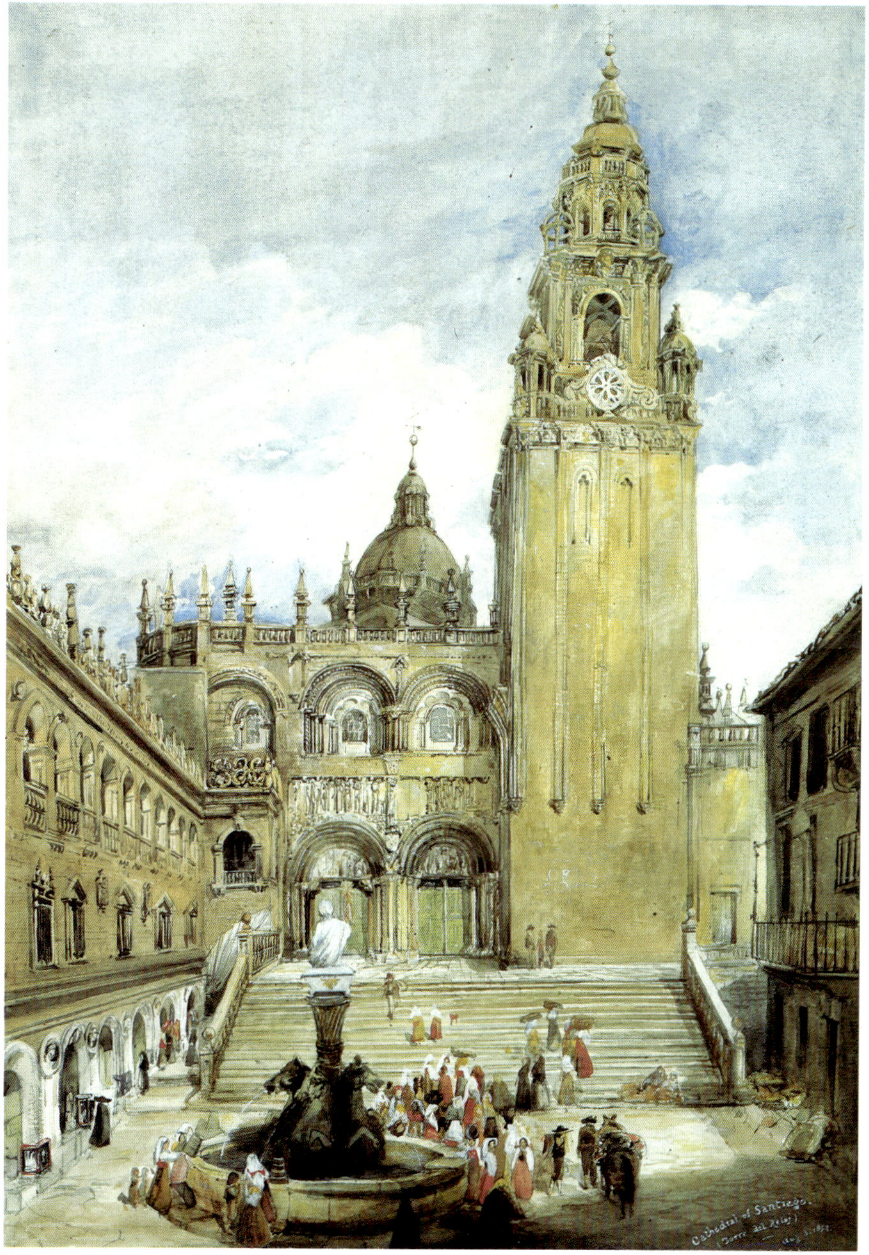

on 2 August. In a letter of 4 August 1852 Lady Canning told her aunt, Lady Caledon, that they 'had set their hearts on getting to this curious old place & at last we accomplished it by diligence. We rather grudged travelling through the night in such a beautiful country, but we could see it very well by a full moon & when the sun got high next day & the 8 mules kicked up clouds of dust, we were quite of the mind that night travelling only wd do here – & accordingly this very night we start to go back to meet the yacht at Corunna. This is a most curious place. Magnificent buildings, convents & churches & a grand cathedral all in complete decadence, yet 20,000 people they say were here last week for St James's day. Pilgrims & amateurs of Bullfights. We have had much trouble to be lodged what with the remnants of this crowd & the very scanty measure of service that we are glad to have escaped the feast'.

In 1846 one of the Maids of Honour, Eleanor Stanley, had particularly admired Lady Canning's Spanish and Greek sketches, but when, in November 1852, she saw the new watercolours, including those of Santiago, she thought them the 'best I have ever seen of hers' *(Twenty Years at Court, Memoirs & letters of the Hon. Eleanor Stanley,* ed. Mrs Steuart Erskine (1916), pp. 121, 221).

The South Coast and the Château d'Eu 1843

QUEEN VICTORIA AND PRINCE ALBERT cruised along the south coast from 28 August to 2 September in their new royal yacht, the *Victoria and Albert.* Lady Canning was pleased when the dates of her period in Waiting were changed so that she should accompany the royal party on this hastily arranged trip, first ' to all the sea ports & the new steam yacht is being prepared in a great hurry for it. I shall like that much better than a month of Windsor – but I am already getting puzzled to think how I am to fit up clothing that will suit Court & sea combined'. Lady Canning told her mother that the Queen was 'in high spirits at the thought of an expedition'. During the trip along the coast Lady Canning had to admit in her travel diary that there were some considerable physical difficulties in being a Lady in Waiting: 'I s^{hd} like to see many of my friends accept the post of Lady in Waiting' for you had to get in and out of carriages, boats and barges with seldom anyone to hand you out, because the Queen went first, then Prince Albert '& me next – so every one but he is too far off to lend a hand – & it is necessary to be active' and wherever they went there was 'perpetual firing' and for anyone frightened in a carriage there were 'mobs' and 'scrambling, kicking horses' (Canning papers).

It was next arranged that the royal party should cross the Channel to visit Louis-Philippe, King of the French, at the Château d'Eu in Normandy from 2 to 7 September. It was the Queen's first trip abroad. She was delighted with it, and especially glad to meet the 'French family' and she 'pleased them all very much'. Lady Canning thought it 'a most amusing visit'.

Sidmouth
Lent by H.M. Queen Elizabeth II (RL 20197: DM 707)
Watercolour with white heightening. 10.6 x 22 cm
Inscribed and obscurely dated, not by the artist,
Sidmouth August

Sidmouth
Watercolour with white heightening. 8 x 22 cm *(opposite)*
Dated and inscribed *1843 / Sidmouth August: 30* and on the mount *Sidmouth from on board the Victoria & Albert August 30. 1843*

On 30 August as the yacht sailed past Sidmouth the Queen asked Lady Canning to sketch it for her as it was the place where her father, the Duke of Kent, had died in 1820. The version painted for the Queen is more elaborate with a number of boats at sea.

Dartmouth
Watercolour with white heightening. 10.6 x 16.3 cm
Dated and inscribed on mount *Dartmouth. Augst 30.*

Lady Canning was on duty as Lady in Waiting when Queen Victoria made her first voyage along the south coast in the new royal yacht, from 28 August to 2 September 1843. They 'coasted along Dorsetshire, Devonshire, passed Lyme Regis, Axmouth, Sidmouth, Exmouth, Torbay & Torquay, – undulating coast with very high cliffs, and beautifully wooded valleys'. A cow was retained on board to provide fresh milk for the royal party. A sheep was given to the Queen at Portland 'but she has taken an affection to it, & it is not to be killed as long as she is on board'. They 'went in to Dartmouth – a lovely spot; high hills, with rocks, & trees, and a narrow deep winding river; at the entrance an old Fort, & church built on a rock... The water was covered with boats: every thing had a holiday look – bells ringing, guns firing, re-echoed still louder by the rocks – flags on every steeple, and every vessel dressed. The Queen rowed up the river in the barge for a short distance and we proceeded afterwards to Plymouth' (Canning papers).

In Lady Canning's version of this view the buildings are a little different from those in the version painted for the Queen (also dated 30 August, RL 20159), and there are fewer boats.

Château d'Eu: a char-à-banc driving up
Lent by H.M. Queen Elizabeth II (RL 20009: DM 709. From Souvenir Album I, 50)
Watercolour. 20 x 28.4 cm
Inscribed on mount *The Château d'Eu, Sept 3rd. 1843*

The garden side of the château with a char-à-banc and six horses driving to the right.

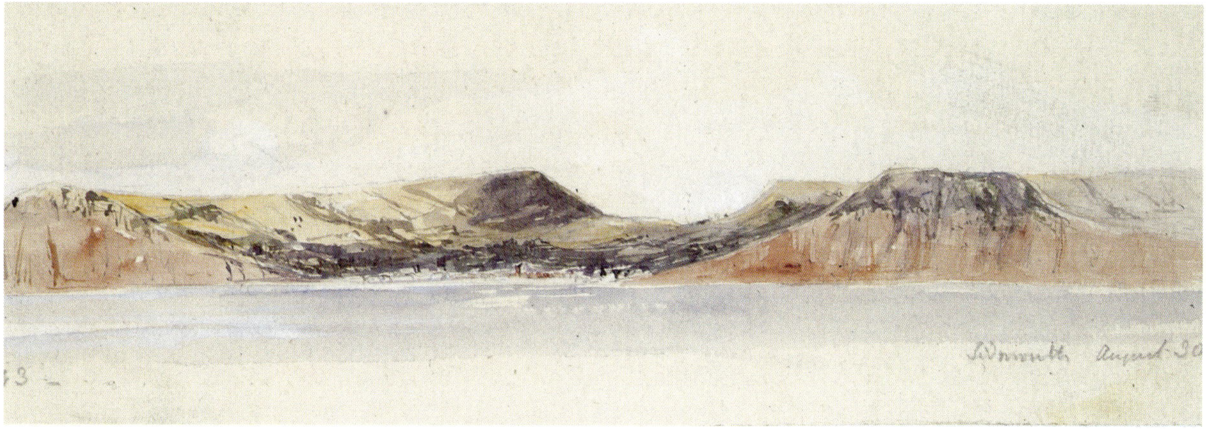

Sidmouth.

Château d'Eu: a char-à-banc driving up
Pencil with grey wash and white heightening
16.5 x 32.3 cm
Dated and inscribed on the mount *Chateau d'Eu, Sept 3.*

The château had been built in 1578, but was enlarged by King Louis-Philippe. Here the royal party are seen driving in two of the King's char-à-bancs. Lady Canning found them 'the most wonderful carriages, a mixture between one of Louis XIV's time and a marketting cart from Hampton Court', but the seats were high and without backs and the springs were rough, and she found expeditions very tiring. 'The body was like an enormous coach with a good deal of gilding & coats of arms & containing 2 or 3 rows of seats – the top was flat & supported with little pillars with draperies & curtains of flowery chintz'.

On 6 September, their last day at Eu, the Queen sent for Lady Canning before breakfast to know 'whether I had drawn anything & to bespeak a sketch of the house from the Avenue'. After lunch, as soon as they could get away, Lady Canning, with the Maid of Honour, 'rushed with drawing materials to the Avenue, and got through our ordered sketches'. This drawing was worked up in watercolour for the Queen (RL 20009).

Château d'Eu: parterre and gardens.

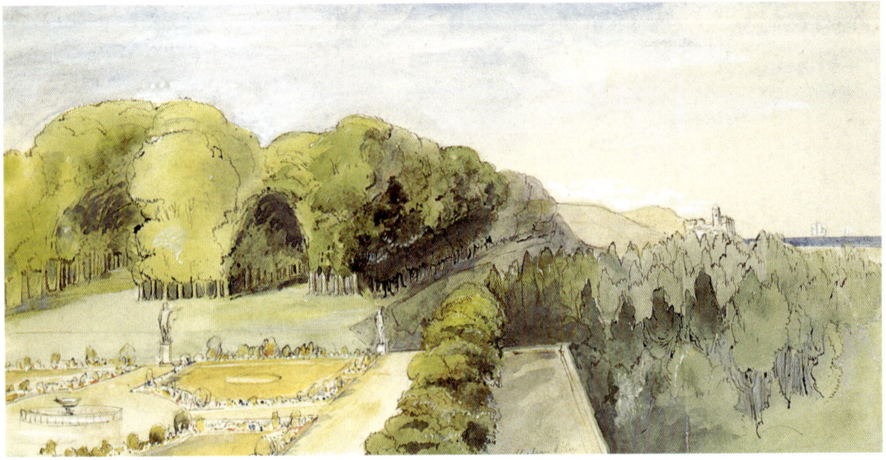

Château d'Eu: parterre and gardens
Lent by H.M. Queen Elizabeth II (RL 20012: DM 711. From Souvenir Album I, 52b)
Watercolour. 15.5 x 23.4 cm
Signed, dated and inscribed *Chateau D'Eu / Sept 5th 1843* and *Gardens of Chateau D'Eu / C.C.Sept 1843*

The drawing at Harewood shows the same subject as this watercolour, but combined with another in the Royal Collection (RL 20010) which continues the composition to the right to include the view of Le Tréport. More figures, soldiers and horses are shown in the Queen's watercolour.

Château d'Eu: parterre and gardens
Watercolour, bodycolour with white heightening.
19.7 x 37.1 cm
Inscribed *at Chateau d'Eu* and on the mount *from the Chateau d'Eu Sept.5*

Showing the parterre with the avenues, and Le Tréport on the right, where they had landed. Probably drawn from Lady Canning's room which was above the Queen's suite, on the garden side of the château ('I could not be better lodged'), and elaborated in the Queen's version. Lady Canning wrote in her diary for 5 September: 'As usual began the day with a private breakfast at $^1/_2$ past 7. Drew one of the views from my window'. The Queen expected Lady Canning to make watercolours for her, and inquired to make sure these were being done.

Visit to Germany

QUEEN VICTORIA AND PRINCE ALBERT travelled to Germany in August 1845 to visit the Prince's homeland. On 11 August they reached Brühl by railway to stay with King Frederick William IV of Prussia. Three days later the party travelled on to Schloss Stolzenfels, which stood in a splendid position overlooking the Rhine. The Queen enjoyed staying in the 'bijou of a castle' and noted that Lady Canning was 'sketching delightfully'. However, it was cramped for the hundred and ten guests who were staying in the castle, and forty others had to be put up in the town below. Lady Canning told her mother that the Queen was 'very much pleased with her reception & enchanted with Germany & Albert is as proud as possible showing her everything' (Canning papers).

The party travelled on to Coburg and, from 19 to 27 August, stayed at the Rosenau, outside the town, 'Albert's birthplace & favourite home'. On August 27 they moved on towards Gotha, staying the night at Schloss Reinhards-brunn, eight miles from the town.

Schloss Brühl: view of the parterre
Pencil with white heightening. 27.3 x 37.5 cm
Inscribed on the mount *Garden of the Palace of Bruhl*

The Queen and Prince Albert stayed at Schloss Brühl with King Frederick William IV of Prussia from 11 to 14 August 1845 before going on to Schloss Stolzenfels. Lady Canning made a watercolour and this drawing, probably from her window, and later made a copy of this for the Queen's Album. She had much trouble with her perspective and, the following February, told her mother: 'You will be glad to hear that my drawings pass muster very decently in the book. They are not yet properly stuck in, but they do not look near so bad as I feared & they have given complete satisfaction, particularly that one of Bruhl gardens which is admired for that very perspective which troubled us so much – so I hope it is right'.

Schloss Stolzenfels
Pencil with white heightening. 24.9 x 35.4 cm
Inscribed on drawing *Stolzenfels* and dated and inscribed on the mount *Castle of Stolzenfels on the Rhine / belonging to the King of Prussia. / Sketched during the Queen's visit. August. 15 1845.*

This ruined castle on the Rhine, near Ehrenbreitstein, had been presented to the King of Prussia in 1823 and by 1842 had been restored to plans by K.F.Schinkel, and furnished in the Gothic style by King Frederick William IV of Prussia. Queen Victoria and Prince Albert travelled from Bonn by steamer and stayed at the castle from 14 to 16 August 1845. Lady Canning told her mother: 'This castle is quite small & very difficult to get at, but the views are perfectly lovely & the furniture & fittings up are good – the outside does not look solid enough & is not in such good taste...The K & Q of the Belgians are here too - but they & most of the party are lodged in the Coblentz palace – & have to toil up the hill here each day'. Lady Canning made a similar drawing for the Queen (RL 20415).

Schloss Callenberg from the park
Lent by H.M. Queen Elizabeth II (RL 20583: DM 722. From Souvenir Album III, 23)
Watercolour. 25.3 x 36 cm
Inscribed on the mount *Callenberg 1843*

On 21 August 1845 the royal party visited Callenburg, another castle belonging to the Dukes of Saxe-Coburg-Gotha, a few miles outside Coburg. Having made a quick sketch Lady Canning later painted this watercolour for the Queen, where the steepness of the perspective has been

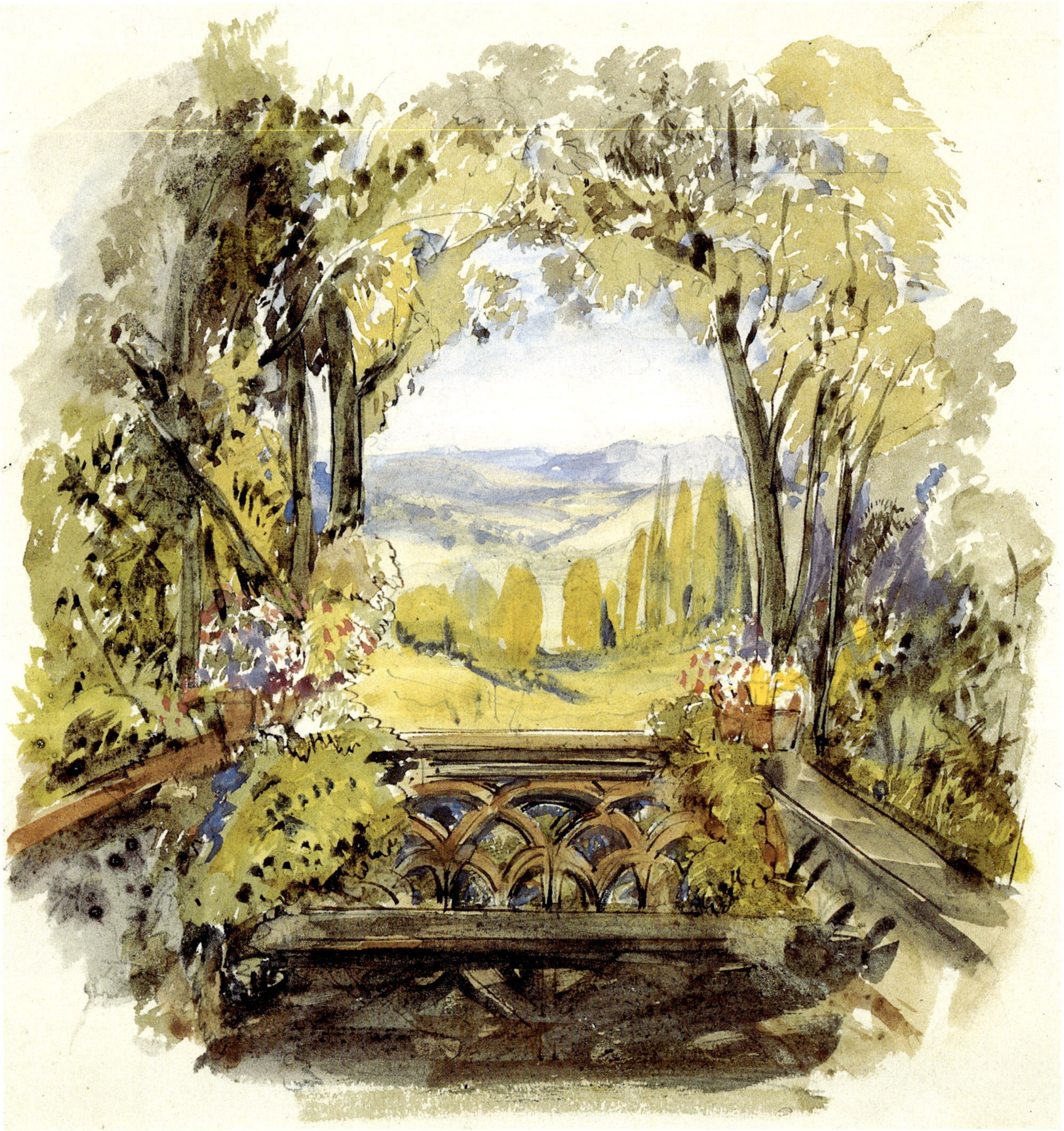

intensified and the area occupied by the castle on the hill top has been narrowed. Flowers have been added on the left as well as more trees.

Schloss Callenburg from the park
Sepia ink, grey wash and white heightening.
24.2 x 34.8 cm
Inscribed *The Calenberg near Coburg.*

Presumably, while at the castle on 21 August 1845, Lady Canning had only time to make this sketch in pencil, which she finished later.

The Rosenau from the Swiss Cottage
Watercolour. 17.8 x 23.9 cm
Inscribed on the drawing *Rosenau / from the / Swiss Cottage* and on the mount *Swiss cottage at Rosenau nr Coburg / August. 1845.*

The royal party stayed at the Rosenau, Prince Albert's birthplace, from 19 to 27 August 1845. This view shows the house from the balcony of the Swiss Cottage, built in the grounds. The Rosenau had been extensively restored by Prince Albert's father, Ernest I, Duke of Saxe-Coburg, between 1806 and 1817. The Prince's brother, Ernest II, and his wife stayed in the Swiss Cottage during the royal visit. On 25 August Lady Canning was glad to note in her diary that: 'I had a holiday & was let to go & draw all day by myself till the 5 o'clock dinner. I first explored the Swiss farm where the Duchess is living and afterwards attempted to get up to an old Castle burnt in a war between Coburgh! and Gotha! The day was beautiful & very hot' (Canning papers).

The Terrace at the Rosenau
Watercolour. 19.3 x 17.3 cm
Inscribed on mount *at Rosenau*

Vignetted view taken from the east terrace outside the Rosenau, looking towards the the village of Mönchröden. A more elaborate version, not vignetted, was painted for Queen Victoria.

Schloss Reinhardsbrunn: the entrance courtyard
Watercolour with white heightening. 33.2 x 23.5 cm
Inscribed on the mount *Rheinhardsbrun in the Thuringian Forest / belonging to the Duke of Coburg*

Opposite: The Terrace at the Rosenau.

Below: The Rosenau from the Swiss Cottage.

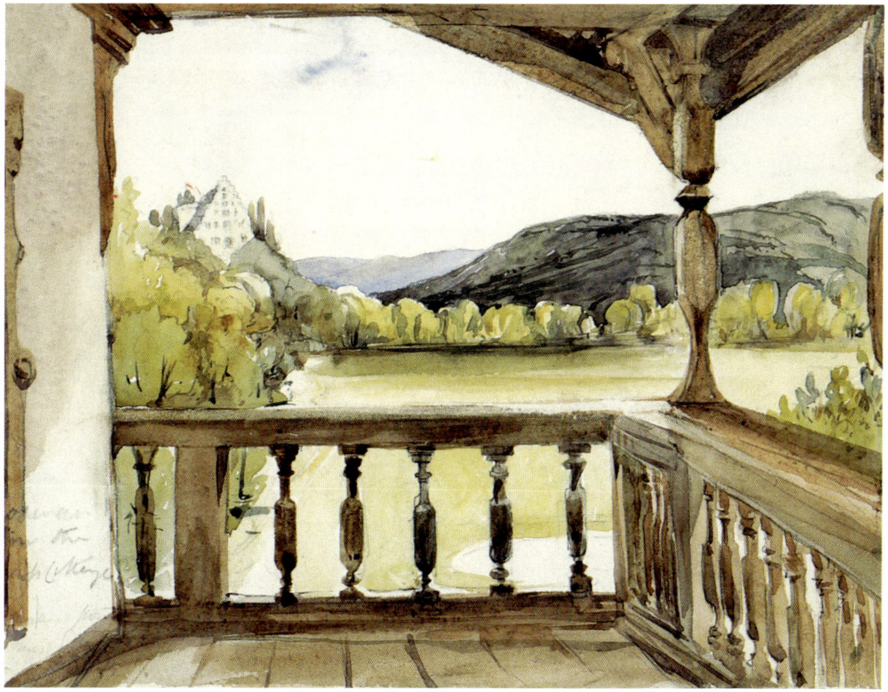

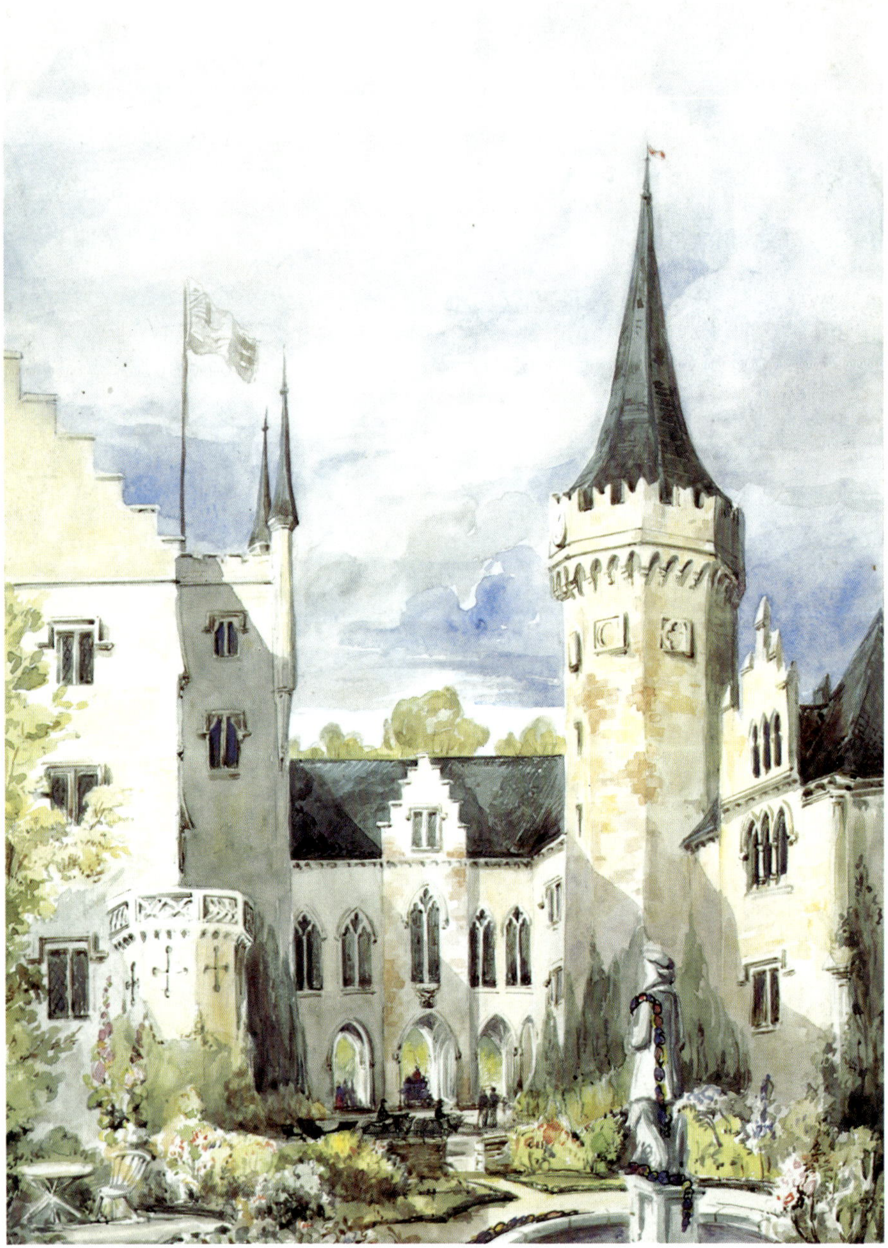

The entrance to the castle with the terrace outside with, on the right, a fountain with the statue of a huntsman with his dog, decorated with laurels. A carriage drives up in the middle distance.

The summer residence of the Dukes of Saxe-Coburg-Gotha, in Thuringia, where Queen Victoria and Prince Albert stayed for a night on 27 August and returned on 2 September. Described by Lady Canning as 'once a convent but rebuilt in an odd Gothic style by the late Duke. It is very well furnished & very comfortable & well kept, but must be only a summer place for it is surrounded by ponds & hills covered with forests of spruce & silver fir all round'. Duke Ernest I was a keen builder, as were many of the Saxe-Coburg family, and delighted in restoring and improving the family houses. Reinhardsbrunn 'was his last creation'.

On 28 August Lady Canning described how they had a 'quiet morning at Reinhardsbrunn & were able to draw & walk about in the woods... The grounds are nicely kept and there are gay beds very full of gaudy & common flowers. I observed one odd device in a little pond decorated all round with wreaths of flowers – there was in the middle the pedestal of a statue. A fountain gushed out of each side of it and fell into the middle of a wreath of dahlias sunk about 2 inches under the water - looking as if under glass & causing pretty reflections of the colours of the flowers'.

On their return to Reinhardsbrunn on 2 September Lady Canning thought 'it was quite a pleasure to spend 2 more hours in the pretty place on such a lovely day. I was begged by the Queen to draw which I was obliged against my will to do, & found a quiet corner & made a bad scribble which, like all I have done this journey, she intends to paste into her book' (Canning papers). The Queen was delighted with all Lady Canning's efforts and particularly praised them for being 'so like the places' (Journal, 11 September 1845).

Visits to Scotland

QUEEN VICTORIA AND PRINCE ALBERT made three visits to Scotland, in 1842, 1844 and 1847, before they rented Balmoral Castle in 1848. On their second visit in 1844 they stayed with Lord and Lady Glenlyon at Blair Castle. Their second son, Prince Alfred, had been born on 6 August, and they travelled north on 9 September. Lady Canning was relieved to find that 'the Queen likes being here very much, certainly I was afraid it was an experiment that might not succeed but it certainly has turned out well'. When they left she felt that the Queen 'has been very happy & the visit has answered very well' (Canning papers). The Queen found that 'after the constant trying publicity, we are accustomed to, it is so pleasant & refreshing, to be able, amidst such beautiful surroundings, to enjoy such complete privacy & such a simple life' (Journal, 16 September 1844).

While she was staying at Blair Castle the Queen gave her permission that Lord Glenlyon's Atholl Highlanders should serve as her bodyguard. They consisted of 'a large number of men about 150 or 200 who are all volunteers. They do their exercises beautifully, & are in full Highland dress and armed with Lochaber axes, claymores & dirks & pistols. The chiefs all belong to Ld Glenlyon & once a year they have a field day & otherwise turn out only on great occasions. There are 5 tents for them in the front of the castle and 24 men & 2 officers are on guard for each three days. These sentries are so picturesque & so well suited to the country – the group standing about the little camp is always quite beautiful'.

On 16 September Lady Canning noted that 'there will be a great deal to draw here for the Queen wants views done for her in every direction', and a week later the Queen was delighted that 'Lady Canning has been making numbers of pretty little sketches of the scenery about here, for me' (Journal, 24 September 1844). The Lord Chamberlain, Lord Breadalbane, arranged that Charles Landseer, the brother of Edwin, should be sent for to draw scenes of the royal visit. Lady Canning records that 'he is not at all pleased with the subject & fidgetted about a great deal while doing nothing'. He finally did draw the subject, but Lady Canning drew it also for herself, but not for the Queen. 'It was quite a Landseer picture all the tents & the Highlanders on Guard for a background the dead deer & the pony standing by him a number of picturesque kilted keepers' (Canning papers, 18 September 1844).

William Leitch, who had been teaching Lady Canning in the south, was also invited to come to Blair Castle and, unlike Charles Landseer, was 'delighted with his orders & says he will make a great number of pretty drawings from the subjects I shewed him' (Canning papers).

Opposite: Schloss Reinhardsbrunn.

Below: Blair Castle with the Atholl Highlanders mounting guard (see page 22).

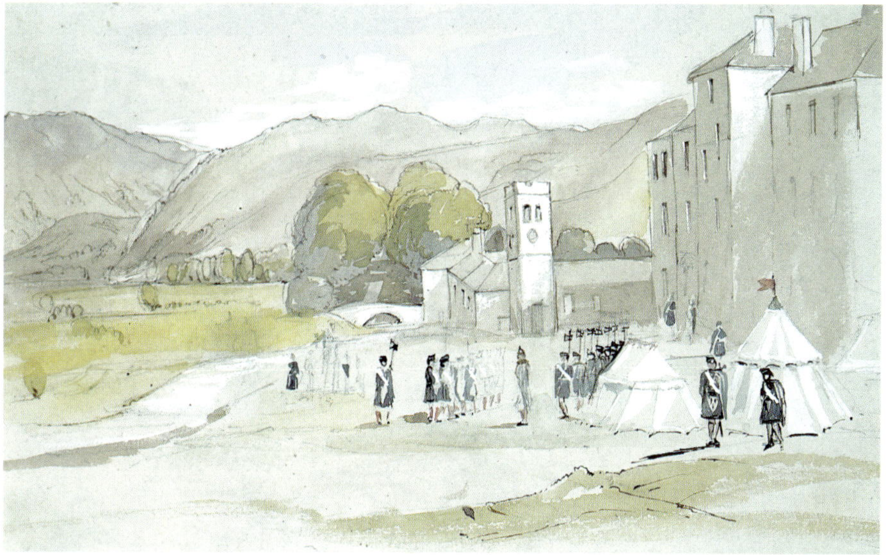

Blair Castle, with the Atholl Highlanders mounting guard

Watercolour with white heightening. 18.9 x 30.4 cm

Inscribed on the mount *Blair Castle. when inhabited by the Queen. / The Athole Highlanders mounting Guard*

Lord and Lady Glenlyon lent the castle to the Queen and Prince for their visit from 11 September to 1 October 1844. Lady Canning's view is drawn from near the point from which Charles Landseer drew it for the Queen in 1844, and William Evans drew it for the Duchess of Kent in 1850. It shows the castle on the right, the church and the encampment of the Atholl Highlanders in the foreground.

On the River Tilt

Watercolour. 30.4 x 20.2 cm

Dated and inscribed on the mount *On the Tilt Sept. 1844*

Painted very much in the style of William Leitch, who had been teaching Lady Canning before she went to Scotland, and was also at Blair painting watercolours for the Queen in a similar style at the same time.

On 8 September Lady Canning wrote that as it was 'another beautiful day I made one or two slight sketches in Glen Tilt & ran home late to luncheon'. On another occasion she describes one of the hazards of sketching *en plein air*. She was 'determined to be out early & to have a long drawing morning', so she set off on 'the old pony', saddled and bridled, with a groom following on foot. He was left far behind so Lady Canning pointed out her route and went on ahead, but the cockney groom mistook her directions. She tied the pony to a fence while she made a sketch, but some horses in the next field 'had been bullying him – and somehow soon after leading him along I let go the bridle & off he was. The rattling of my bag of paint-boxes & pencils kept him going & I had a full half hour's chase till the bag was thrown & he stood still & I caught him & did get another sketch tying him safe up to a tree' (Canning papers).

THE ISLE OF ARRAN AND ARDVERIKIE

Queen Victoria travelled up the west coast in August 1847 to stay at Ardverikie on Loch Laggan. She passed the Isle of Arran on 17 August and drew Brodick Castle, but Lady Canning was not in attendance on this occasion. She had visited the island in September 1846 and was asked by the Queen to work up for her the watercolour she had made at that time. The drawing she offered the Queen turned out to be too large for the Souvenir Album, but the Queen kept it (it hangs at Balmoral) and Lady Canning was asked to make a smaller one for the Album (Canning papers).

In 1844 the Marquis of Abercorn had leased from Macpherson of Cluny the land upon which he built the shooting-box, Ardverikie, which he lent to the Queen in 1847. During her visit she had almost continual bad weather, but whenever it was fine, she sketched with Lady Jocelyn, another of her Ladies in Waiting.

Almost the entire house was destroyed by fire in 1873, including sketches by Landseer on the walls. It was rebuilt in the later 1870s.

Brodick Castle, Isle of Arran

Sepia ink with sepia and grey-blue wash and white heightening. 24.4 x 35.5 cm

Inscribed and dated on the mount *Arran / Brodick Castle / Sept 46*

The Cannings were friends of William, Marquis of Douglas, and his wife, the former Princess Marie of Baden (whom he married in 1843). They stayed at Brodick on

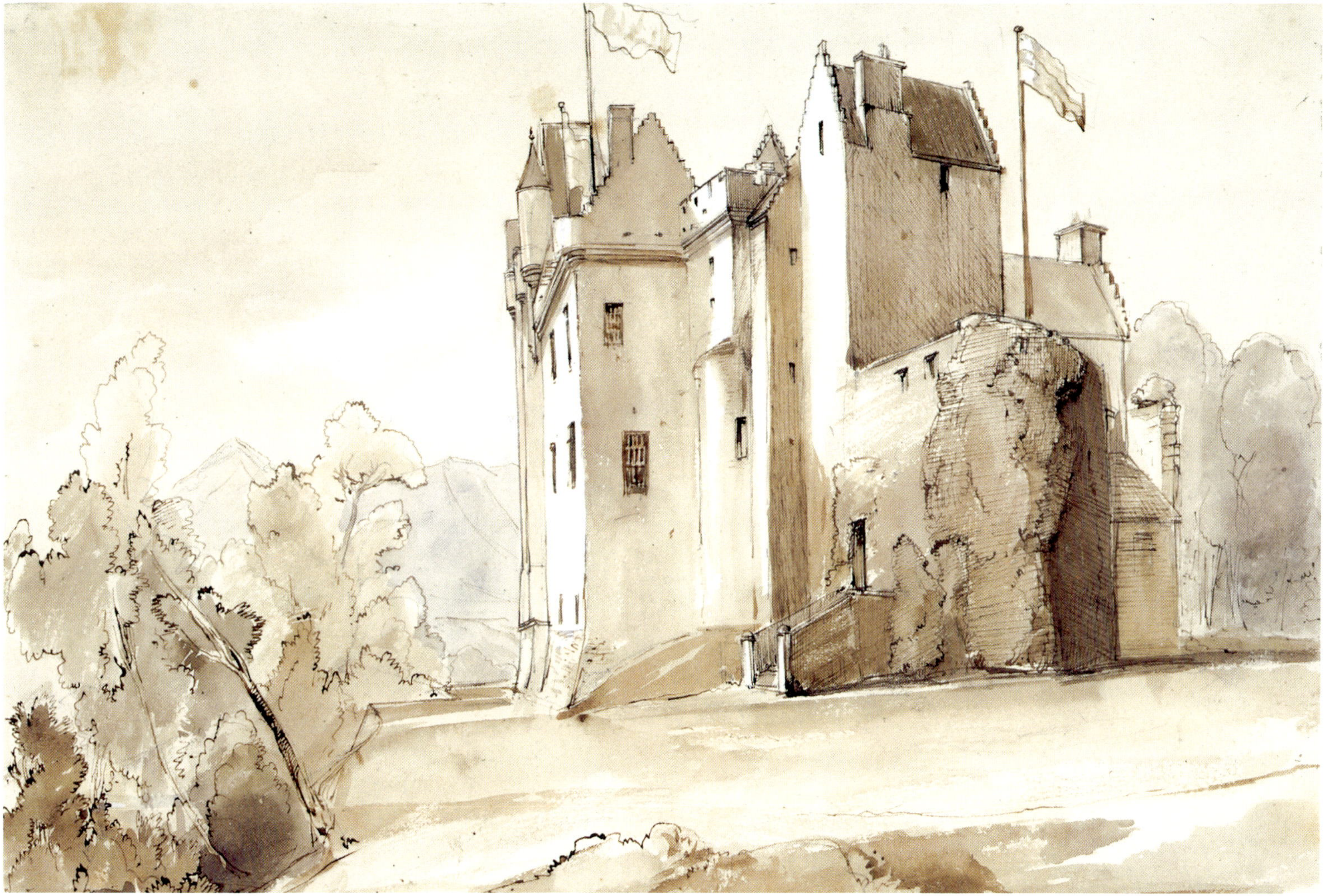

Brodick Castle (see page 22).

several occasions, including 1846, 1851 and 1852. The castle was restored and extended by Lord Douglas after his marriage, and a wing was added by the architect James Gillespie Graham. Work was unfinished when Queen Victoria visited the castle in 1847, when Lady Canning was not in Waiting, and she made no version of this watercolour for the Queen. A view of the castle, in the Royal Collection, painted for the Duchess of Kent on a visit in 1851 by Inglefield, shows the completed castle.

Brodick Bay, Isle of Arran: looking up Glen Rosa
Lent by H.M. Queen Elizabeth II (RL 20203: DM 741. From Souvenir Album IV, 33)
Watercolour with white heightening. 25.4 x 35 cm.

Ardverikie.

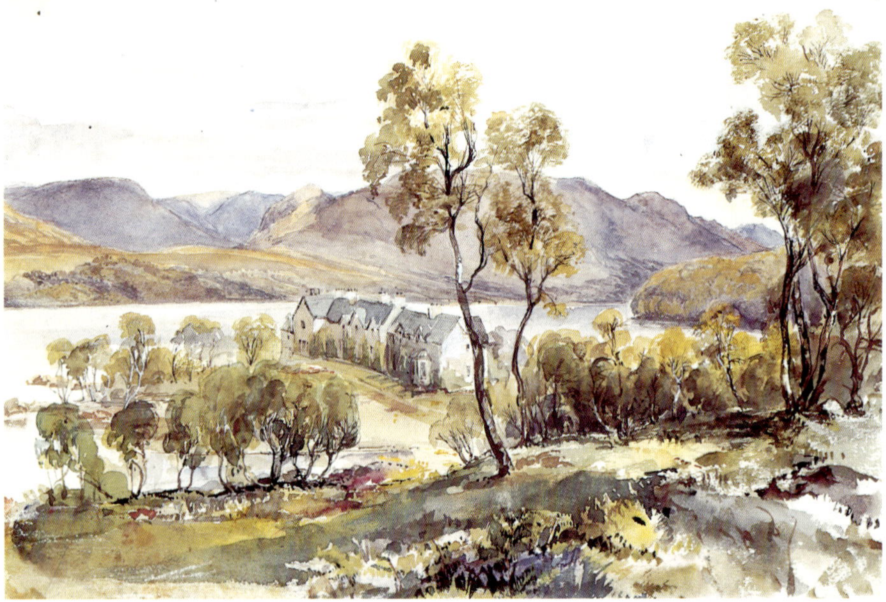

Dated in a later hand *17 Aug /47,* inscribed on the mount *Isle of Arran*

Much more elaborate than Lady Canning's own study, with figures and with much more detail in the foreground on the left.

Brodick Bay, Isle of Arran: looking up Glen Rosa
Pencil and colour wash. 25.4 x 35.5 cm
Inscribed on mount *Brodick Bay looking up Glen Rosa*
Verso: pencil sketches

A study made in September 1846 and used as a basis for the watercolour in the Royal Collection.

Ardverikie
Watercolour and bodycolour. 24.9 x 34.7 cm
Inscribed on the mount *Ardverikie*

The Queen described this house, lent to her by the Marquis of Abercorn, as a comfortable shooting-box, five miles from the nearest house. Prince Albert told the Duchess of Kent that it was 'very lonely and wild...The reporters call it an "un-come-at-able place", because they are quartered on the other side of Loch Laggan, which is only to be crossed on a flying bridge, that belongs exclusively to ourselves' *(Letters of the Prince Consort 1831-1861,* ed K.Jagow (1938), p.116). While the Queen was staying at Ardverikie in August 1847 Lady Canning was staying at Achnacarry with the 3rd Earl and Countess of Malmesbury from 16 July. Achnacarry belonged to Cameron of Lochiel but was rented by Lord Malmesbury each autumn from 1844. Lady Canning also complained of the bad weather: 'two days we could not get out at all & many other times we have been drenched to the skin. I am afraid Laggan will not have answered for the Queen, for ever since she arrived there it has been bad weather' – she reported that 'people said they had not had as much rain as lately, for 9 years' (Canning papers).

In September 1848 Lady Canning seems to have stayed with the Abercorns at Ardverikie, and again in August 1849, when Edwin Landseer was a fellow guest. She probably painted views for the Queen on this occasion, and the Queen's version of this subject (with variations in the foreground and trees) was reproduced in the illustrated edition of her *Leaves from the Journal of Our Life in the Highlands* (1868) RL 20205.

Loch Laggan
Watercolour. 30.2 x 49.5 cm
Dated and inscribed on the mount *LOCH LAGGAN / 1849.*

The loch on which Ardverikie was situated and presumably drawn while Lady Canning was staying at that house in August 1849. Painted on rough watercolour paper, Lady Canning's style here shows the influence of her lessons from William Leitch.

BALMORAL CASTLE

After the very wet royal holiday in the west of Scotland in 1847 it was decided that, in 1848, they would try Deeside, which their doctor assured them was dry, cold and healthy. The lease of Balmoral Castle had become available on the sudden death of the Earl of Aberdeen's brother, Sir Robert Gordon. His small shooting-box had been recently enlarged when Sir Robert retired from the foreign service. It delighted the Queen and Prince, but as Lady Canning decided: 'This is a small house & would be comfortable with a few people in due proportions, but now, with eight at dinner and the three children, there are sixty servants !... The Queen is a great deal out, and has been drawing, and the Prince takes little walks with her, and then shoots for an hour or two at a time!' Four days later she wrote: 'We have lovely weather & the Queen is more & more delighted with this place & the beautiful country near it'.

In 1852 the estate was acquired for Prince Albert and foundations were laid for a new Castle. The new royal apartments were in use in 1855, and then the old house was demolished.

QUEEN VICTORIA

Copied by the Queen from the watercolour by Lady Canning and given to her.
View in the Corrie Buie
Watercolour and bodycolour. 27 x 41.3 cm *(see page 26)*
Signed *Victoria R. copied from Ly Canning's drawing, Oct 1848*

View in the Corrie Buie
Lent by H.M. Queen Elizabeth II (RL 19461: DM 749. From Souvenir Album IV, 68)
Watercolour and bodycolour with gum arabic. 25.8 x 44.6 cm
Inscribed on the reverse, as by Lady Canning, *Corrie Bowie Sept 19th /48*

Showing the rough hillside near Balmoral known also as Corbhuie or Choire Bhuidhe. On 20 September the Queen saw and admired this 'beautiful spot', where the 'distant hills formed such a fine background' (Journal).

Balmoral: the garden front of the old Castle
Pencil and white heightening. 22.5 x 35.1 cm
Inscribed on the mount *Balmoral*

The old Castle, probably drawn in the late 1840s, before the small tree on the lawn and the heavy foliage over the doorway were removed.

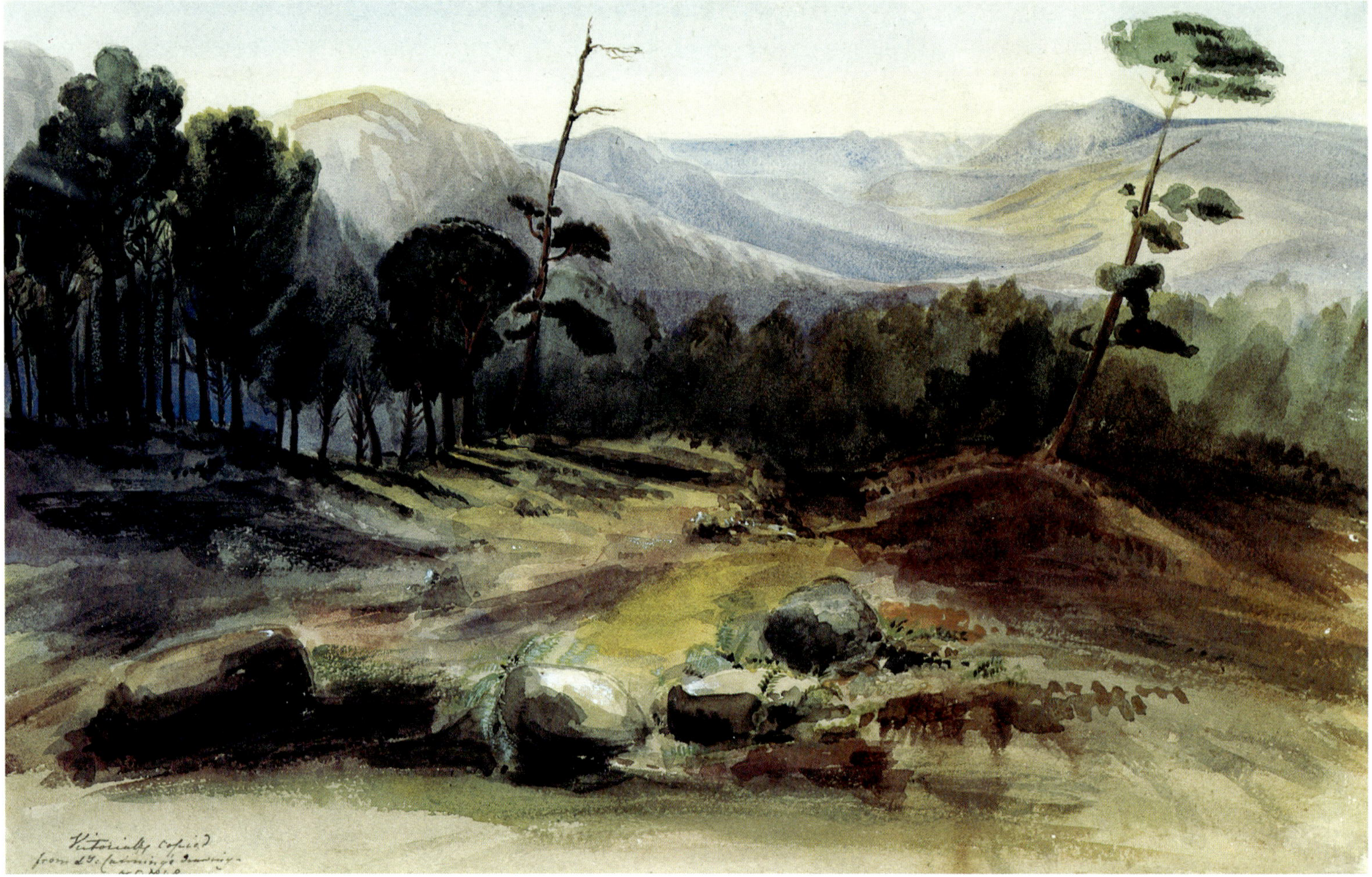

Queen Victoria after Lady Canning: View in the Corrie Buie (see page 25).

Balmoral: the old Castle from the gardens
Watercolour. 22.7 x 27.6 cm
Inscribed on the mount *Balmoral.*

The side of the Castle from the north-east. On her first spell of Waiting at Balmoral Lady Canning told her mother: 'I think this place has succeeded very well it is not very pretty near the house but there are beautiful views near and a great variety of drives'. Attempts to grow flowers near the house were frustrated by deer and rabbits. A week later she complained that she had had no time to write letters because 'I am always at work at *bad* drawings' (Canning papers, 14 and 21 September 1848).

Balmoral: looking up the River Dee
Watercolour and bodycolour. 26.4 x 35.5 cm
Inscribed on the mount *BALMORAL. LOOKING UP THE DEE. 1848.* and *The Quarry*

Balmoral Castle from across the River Dee
Pencil, ink, sepia wash and white heightening.
34.4 x 52 cm
Inscribed *Balmoral / Lochnagar*

Drawn from the flagstaff above Crathie Church and showing the old Castle, the temporary Iron Ballroom, the staff quarters and the game larder. On the hilltop can be seen the Purchase Cairn, erected on 11 October 1852 to celebrate the acquisition of the Balmoral estates; this was probably added later to the watercolour, and to the more elaborate version painted for the Queen (RL 19465), as the cairn was only built on the last day of the Queen's visit.

On 1 October Lady Canning told her mother that it was 'a lovely day & I have to go out & sketch & am merely waiting to get leave to order a carriage' (Canning papers).

Falls of the Garbh Allt
Watercolour and bodycolour with white heightening.
36.6 x 24.6 cm
Inscribed on mount *Falls of the Garevalt*

The stream in the Ballochbuie Forest much visited by the royal party on drives and walks from Balmoral Castle. Mounted in Lady Canning's album under the date 1848.

The Dubh Loch
Pencil, watercolour and white heightening. 25.2 x 35.4 cm
Dated and inscribed *Dubh Loch / 1852* and on the mount *The Dhu Loch. Oct 3.*

A loch, between Loch Muick and the mountain, Lochnagar, visited on expeditions by Queen Victoria.

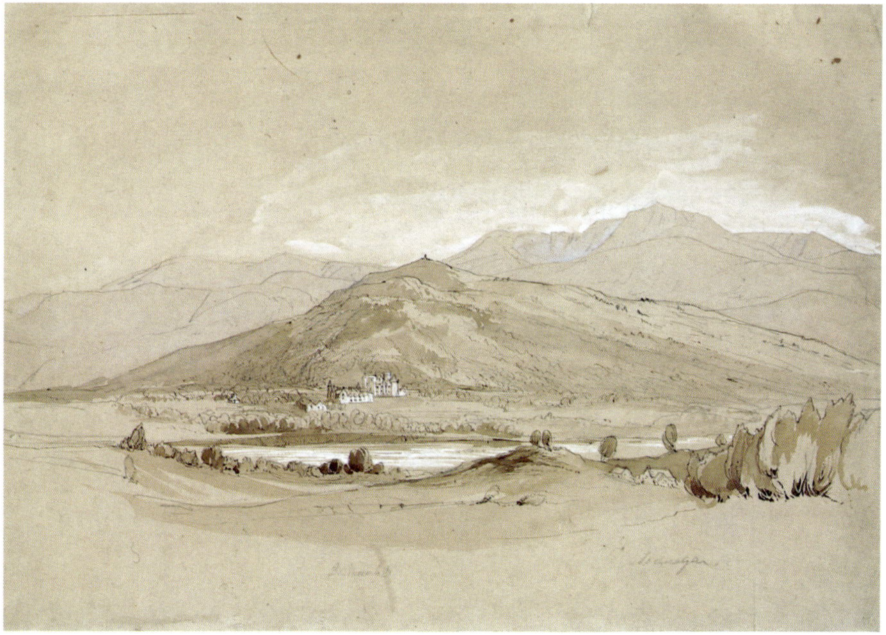

Balmoral Castle from across the River Dee.

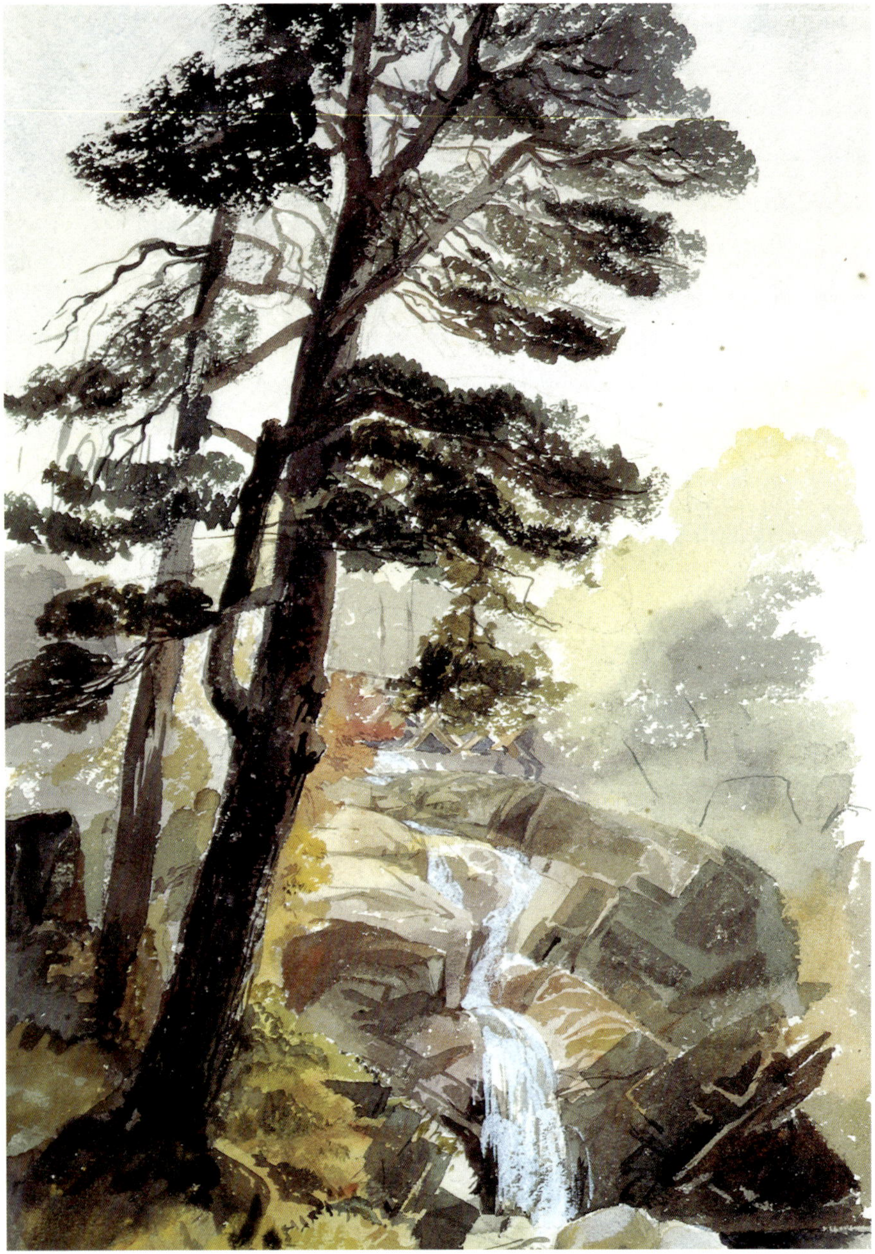

Haddo House: the gardens from the terrace
Watercolour and white heightening. 24.7 x 34.8 cm
Dated and inscribed on the mount *GARDEN AT HADDO HOUSE. / 1848.*

Presumably drawn when the Cannings stayed at Haddo House in Aberdeenshire, with the Earl of Aberdeen, in late September 1848. The grounds were all laid out by Lord Aberdeen and much admired by the Queen when she stayed there in October 1857.

Loch Crinan
Sepia ink, watercolour and white heightening.
24.3 x 45.7 cm
Dated and inscribed *Loch Crinan. / Aug 30. 1852.*

Queen Victoria visited Loch Fyne on 18 August 1847, landed at Lochgilphead and drove through the village to board a handsomely decorated barge to go through the Crinan Canal, with its series of locks, to reach Loch Crinan. On a private visit in 1852 Lady Canning anchored in Loch Crinan on board the *Fair Rosamund* and drew this view. She was at Banavie, near Fort William, on 2 September.

Falls of the Garbh Allt (see page 27).

Osborne House

THE QUEEN AND PRINCE wanted a country home of their own and, in October 1844, they rented Osborne House, a simple eighteenth-century house on the Isle of Wight. The following year they purchased the property, taking possession on 3 April 1845. That year they stayed there from 29 March to 1 April, and each month until September and again in November and December. It was soon decided that the house was too small for their increasing family, so the foundation stone of a new house was laid on 23 June 1845.

The following year, soon after their arrival at Osborne in September 1846, Lady Canning told her grandmother that: 'if we were much used to state anywhere at court, I should think this was an imitation of Trianon. Whatever it is, it perfectly enchants the Queen & Prince & you never saw anything so happy as they are planting their trees with the 5 babes playing about round them'. She tells how the 'flitting into the new house was last Monday – it is rather a Londony place but perfectly comfortable & the views all round are very fine – I remain in the old house and am greatly benefitted by the departure of at least 25 souls. The building is to come down & the foundations of the new part are to be dug immediately'(Canning papers).

Osborne House: the tower of the Royal Pavilion
Pencil with bodycolour and charcoal. 24.2 x 17.4 cm
Dated and inscribed on the mount *Osborne. Sept^{tr}.1846*

The foundation stone of the Pavilion was laid in June 1845. On 14 September 1846 the Queen, who was on board the royal yacht, slept in the Royal Pavilion for the first time. When they left the Queen was 'miserable at having to leave this Paradise, with this perfect house, so soon' (Journal). The Queen and Lady Canning, who was in Waiting, drew the view from the roof on 17 September.

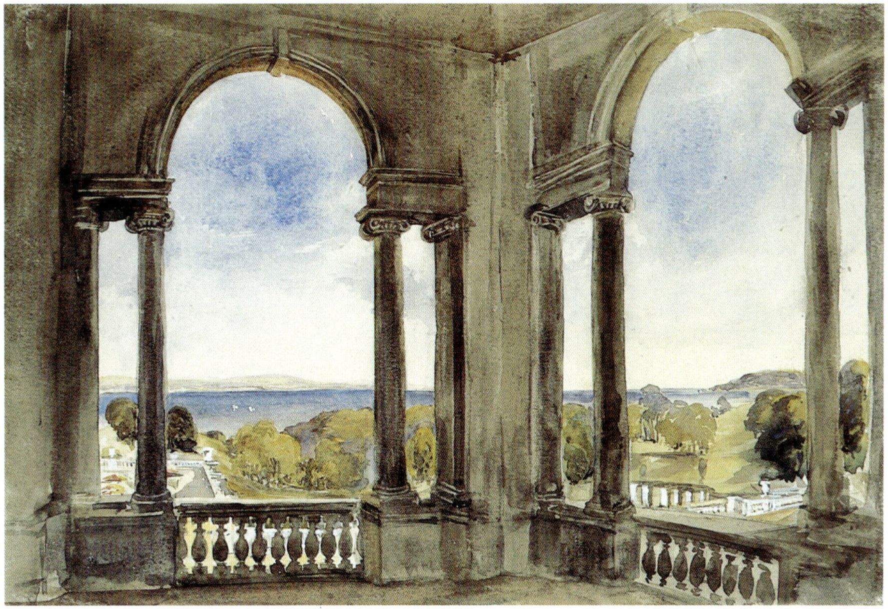

Above: Osborne House: the Solent seen from the Corridor.

Osborne House: view from the gardens
Watercolour. 16.5 x 24.9 cm
Inscribed on mount *Osborne*

The new house, nearing completion.

Osborne House: the Solent seen from the Corridor
Watercolour. 24.6 x 35.5 cm
Dated and inscribed on the mount *OSBORNE. / 1850.*

Drawn from the Grand Corridor, on the first floor, which linked the Main Wing with the Royal Pavilion. Below can be seen the Terrace, with the Vinery on the right, and the Solent in the distance.

Osborne House: the Vinery
Watercolour and bodycolour. 17 x 25.1 cm *(see page 2)*
Dated and inscribed on the mount *Osborne. July / 52*

Lady Canning told Lady Waterford on 7 July 1852 that: 'All these days have been too hot to go out or walk & one saw nothing but detachments of children all about in the arbours & different cool places. They have made really a beautiful garden of terraces with quantities of alcoves & statues but the landscape & rather large formal things are in want of a little setting to rights & I longed to doctor some lines of walk' (Canning papers).

The royal version of this watercolour is signed and dated 5 July 1852 (RL 768). The Vinery, below the Terrace, is newly-built and not yet entirely covered with flowering plants. By 18 July 1854 the Queen described breakfasting on the Terrace 'with the fountains playing and the air perfumed with the smell of orange blossoms, and roses, which quite cover the pergola' (Journal).

Below: Osborne House: view of the Terrace.

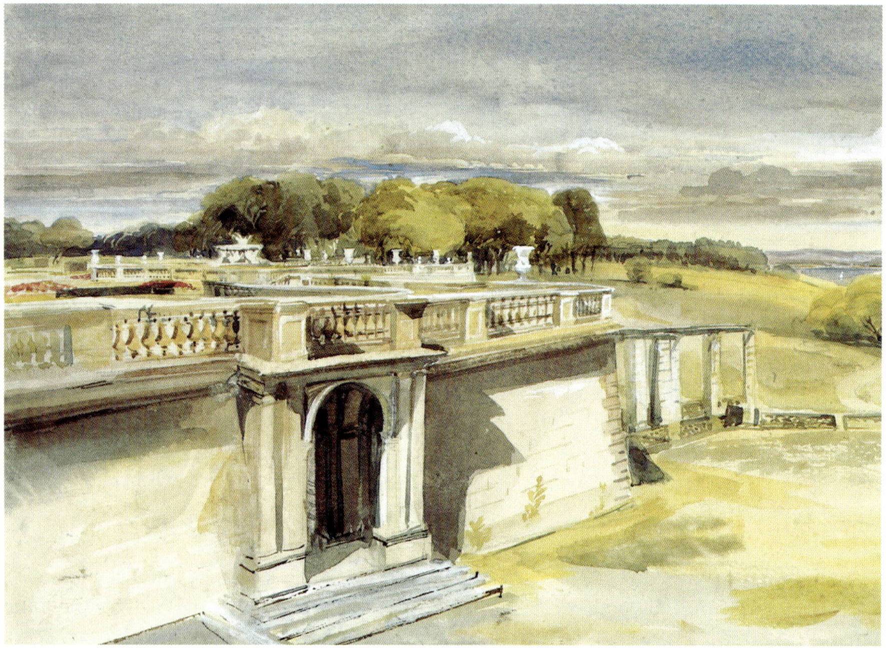

Osborne House: view of the Terrace
Watercolour. 24.8 x 35.5 cm
Dated and inscribed on mount *OSBORNE / 1850*

With a distant view of the Solent. The gardens at Osborne were mainly laid out by Prince Albert. The Terrace laid out in 1848 was completed by the summer of 1849.

Osborne: the Solent seen from the Terrace
Watercolour. 23.2 x 35.5 cm
Inscribed *OSBORNE BY LADY CANNING*

English Views

Memorial to Princess Charlotte at Claremont, Surrey
Pencil with white heightening. 29.7 x 25.9 cm
Dated and inscribed on the mount *Memorial to Princess Charlotte at Claremont / July 1842*

The building was designed by J.W. Hiort and J.B. Papworth in 1816 as a Gothic teahouse with a library for Princess Charlotte who lived at Claremont after her marriage to Prince Leopold of Saxe-Coburg (later Leopold I, King of the Belgians) until her death in 1817. After the death of the Princess the building was completed as a memorial to her, and survived until, in a dilapidated condition, it finally collapsed in the Second World War.

The Revd. Francis Kilverton on a visit to Claremont, in January 1871, described how 'looking down upon the lake through a screening fringe of trees is the old summer arbour of the Princess, a place which she was very fond of and which the King of the Belgians after her death converted into a memorial temple... It is a circular building with small high stained windows emblazoned with the arms of the Royal Houses' *(Kilvert's Diary,* ed. W. Plomer (1938), I, p. 298). As a child and up to the 1840s Queen Victoria stayed on many happy occasions at Claremont ('this *so* very dear old place'; Journal, 10 January 1847). She was there from 9 to 18 July 1842, apparently during Lady Canning's first period in Waiting, and the drawing was probably made then. What especially appealed to the Queen was the lack of formality, and the absence even of sentries on guard when they stayed there. The house was lent to King Louis-Philippe and his family when they were exiled from France in 1848.

Harewood House, Yorkshire
Pencil and white heightening. 17.5 x 24.9 cm

Mounted in the album of drawings dated between 1842 and 1846. Probably drawn on a visit to Harewood House following the marriage, in 1845, of Lady Elizabeth de Burgh, a niece of Lord Canning, to Henry Lascelles, later 4th Earl of Harewood.

One of the earliest views of the house following the rebuilding of the south front by Sir Charles Barry from 1843.

View in Buckingham Palace Garden
Lent by H.M. Queen Elizabeth II (RL 19895: DM 762. From Souvenir Album III, 50)
Pencil and watercolour and white heightening. 35 x 25 cm
Inscribed on the mount *View of Buckingham Palace Garden May 1846*

Lady Canning was in Waiting from 6 May 1846.

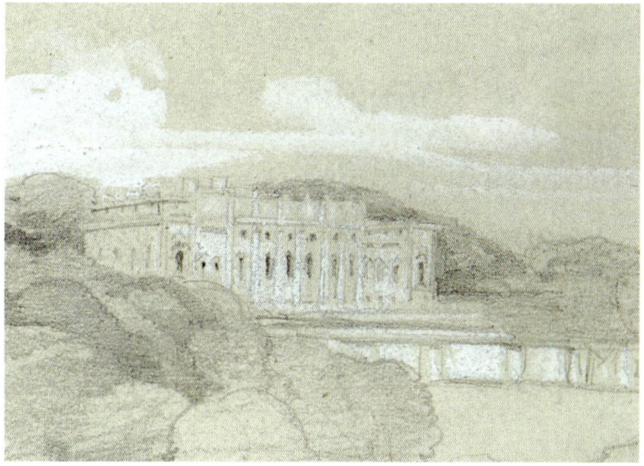

Left: Harewood House (detail). Below: Crystal Palace (see page 32).

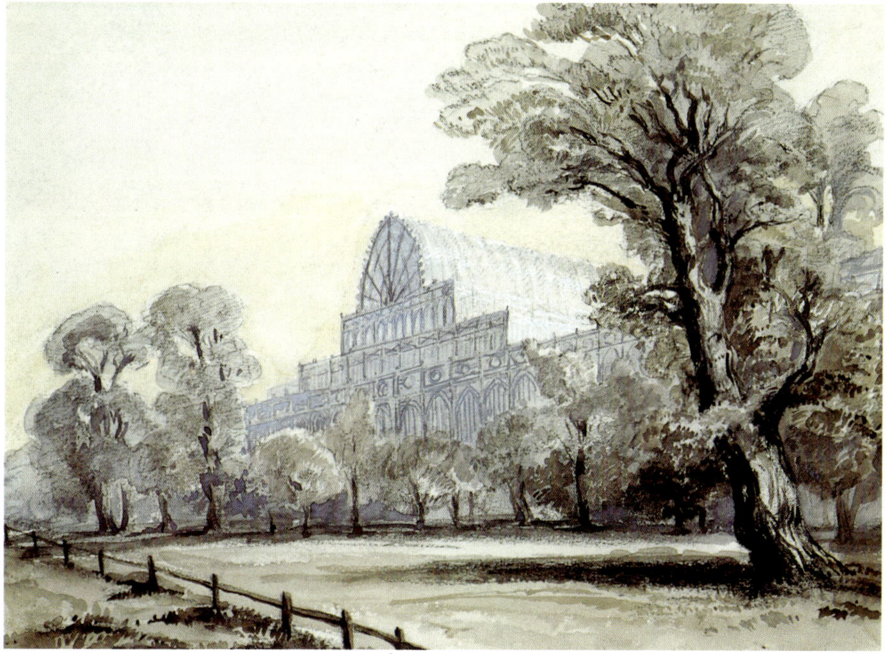

Below: St. Michael's Mount (detail).

Opposite: Temple of Dendera (see page 34).

View in Buckingham Palace Garden
Pencil with white heightening. 35.6 x 25.4 cm
Inscribed on mount *in Buckingham Palace Garden/May 1846*

A preliminary sketch of John Nash's garden front of the Palace, which was much elaborated by Lady Canning in her watercolour for the Queen's album.

Crystal Palace
Pencil, watercolour and bodycolour. 23.3 x 32.2 cm

Presumably drawn in Hyde Park at the time of the Great Exhibition between May and October 1851.

Apparently showing the end of the North Transept with Rotten Row in the foreground, perhaps drawn from a carriage. The popular name for the building was first used in *Punch* on 2 November 1850. Lord Canning was Chairman of the Committee of Jurors and on 15 October reported the Juries' decisions.

The Queen visited the exhibition almost daily until she left London in early July, and on her return in October she made her final daily visits: 'I cannot bear to think it will be over in 3 days. The success has however been enormous' (Journal). On 12 October Lady Canning told her mother that she was going the next day, in attendance on the Queen. However, she had heard that 90,000 tickets had already been given out so that if Lady Stuart planned to be there ' it will not be a comfortable view, but you must be used to the worst of it now as you were there on the most crowded day of all'; that was on 7 October when 109,915 visitors attended. The Queen found it 'as beautiful, bewildering and enchanting as ever' (Journal), and could not bear to think that on 14 October, when she made her final visit, it would be the last time she would 'behold this wonderful creation of my beloved Albert's' (Journal).

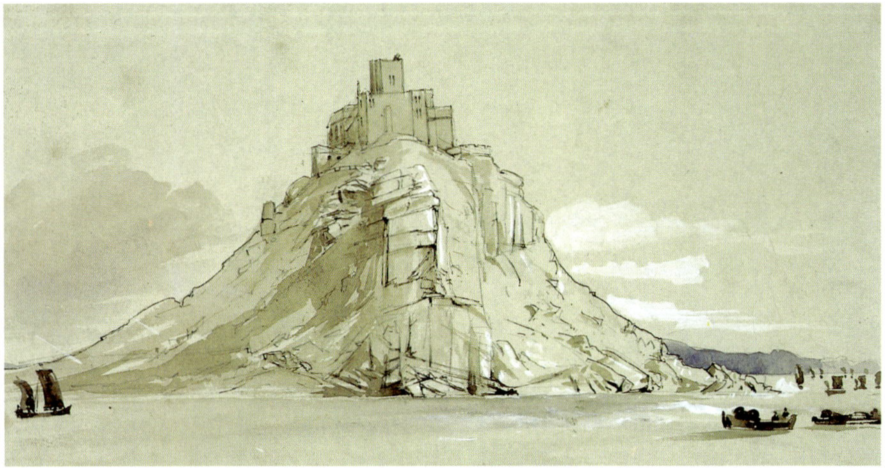

St. Michael's Mount, Cornwall
Sepia ink with sepia and grey-blue washes and white heightening. 22.9 x 34.6 cm
Inscribed *St Michael's Mount Cornwall* and on the mount *August / 53*

When the Queen sailed along the south coast in the royal yacht, she anchored in this bay and visited St Michael's Mount on 5 September 1846. Lady Canning was not in Waiting then, but must have made this sketch before crossing to Ireland in September 1853 to visit the Dublin exhibition with Lord Canning, on their yacht the *Fair Rosamund.*

Mont Orgueil Castle, Jersey
Watercolour and gum arabic. 34.2 x 50.3 cm
Dated and inscribed on mount *Mont Orgueil. Jersey. 1853*

Queen Victoria paid her only visit to Jersey in September 1846 when Lady Canning was not in Waiting. This view was painted on a private visit, perhaps on the same cruise during which Lady Canning drew St Michael's Mount.

The Journey to India

When Lord Canning was appointed Governor-General of India in 1855 Lady Canning realised that there 'are really no reasons, but one's own feelings & dislikes against it & I think it will be that we go'. She felt that had the appointment been for one year 'I w^{d} delight in it – but 5 is terribly long'. On 2 July the Queen 'saw Ly Canning, who, I am grieved to say, has resigned as she is going with Ld Canning to India'. She gave her 'a handsome bracelet with my hair' when she 'took leave of the dear Cannings, with great regret' on 22 November 1855 (Journal).

The Cannings began their journey by travelling in the Sultan's steamboat, *Caradoc,* from Marseilles to Alexandria. From there they went on the new railway line to Cairo, and spent nearly a month in Egypt. Their accommodation and the trip was arranged by Said Pasha, the Egyptian ruler. On 25 December they visited Dendera and on 29-30 December they were at Philae. They travelled as far as the First Cataract by steamer, before joining the ship for India at Suez on 12 January.

After eight days they reached Aden and three days later they arrived at Bombay. Lady Canning wrote at frequent intervals to Queen Victoria, by her request, and described the country and the experiences on their journey. 'Bombay is the most beautiful country with every variety of hill & rock & wood & water. I who so much delight in plants, thoroughly appreciate the beauty of the tropical vegetation whether in the gardens of Bananas & groves of Cocoa nut, or in the wild jungle of Bamboos and magnificent flowering trees and shrubs, & in the 1000 varieties entirely new to me'. Lady Canning became a most subtle flower painter and the splendid watercolours she sent home gave great pleasure. Her mother was 'enchanted with the variety, industry, taste and science' and John Ruskin thought 'they

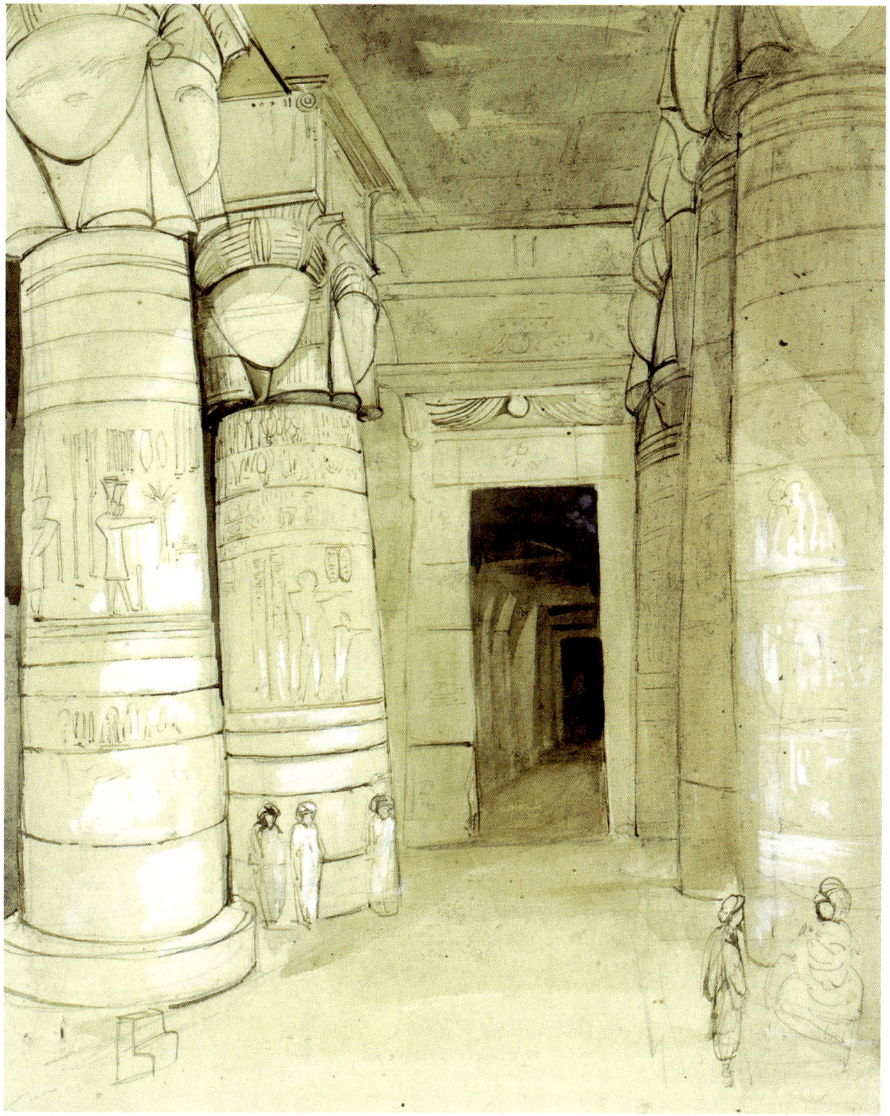

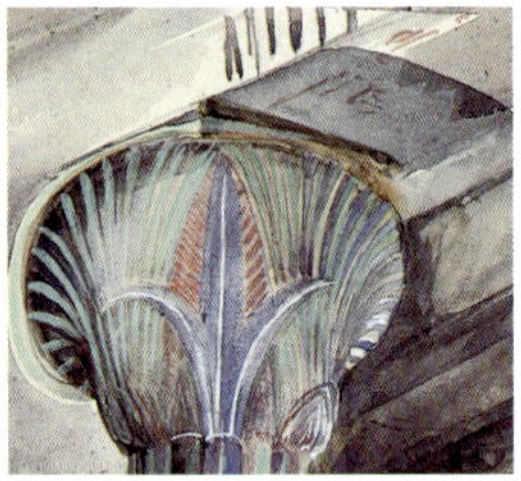

Lady Canning also painted details of capitals. These are from the temples at Philae.

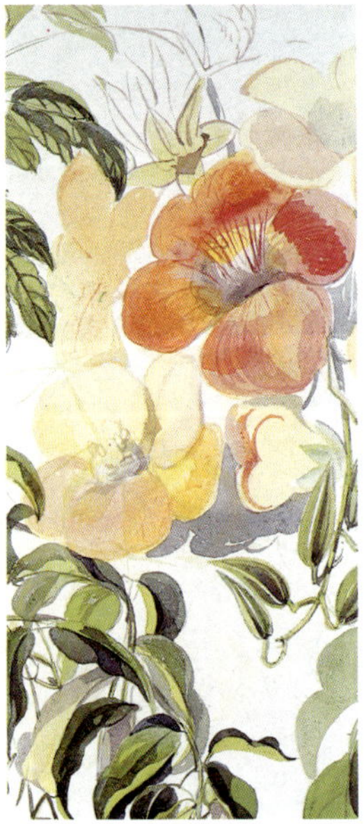

Bignonia, a climbing evergreen, from 'British and Indian Flowers', vol. 1, p.14.

were the greatest representations of flowers he had ever seen'.

Lady Canning noted that the local newspapers were full of their arrival in India: 'I am rather distressed at being announced as a beauty, an artist and an eminent botanist, besides many other things. I fear I shall be found disappointing in all these three lines' (A. Hare, *The Story of Two Noble Lives* (1893), II, p. 17).

However, excellent drawings of plants and flowers and brilliant views of Indian scenery were drawn by Lady Canning in the last five years of her life.

The artist William Simpson, who was working in India, wrote of how 'Lady Canning herself was devoted to art, having been a pupil of W.L. Leitch. She had no family, and to her the march of the camps was principally a sketching tour...In the morning after reaching camp, I generally took a walk to see if there was anything worth sketching, and reported it to Lady Canning, who went out almost every evening to sketch. She had a very large and docile elephant, and could sketch sitting on the howdah. In the evening after dinner I had to show any sketches I had made; Lady Canning produced hers; and any of the officers of the suite who had done anything also produced their work. On account of Lady Canning's interest in art, all who could use the pencil tried their hand, and from this it appeared at times as if the camp was merely a gigantic sketching expedition.' *(The Autobiography of William Simpson R.I.,* ed G. Eyre-Todd (1903), p. 104)

Four months after their arrival in India the Earl of Malmesbury had heard 'a very bad account of Lady Canning whose health seems to be seriously affected by the climate of India'. Nevertheless she did not complain. On 8 November 1861, after her return to Calcutta from an expedition to Darjeeling, she said 'the scenery at Darjeeling had quite repaid her for the journey & the forests were the most magnificent she had ever seen'. Her doctor was worried about her 'great weakness' and inability 'to be rested'. Nevertheless, however weak she felt, she 'busied herself about her room & her drawings' (Ponsonby papers). During the last week of her life Lord Canning seldom left her side and her death from jungle-fever on 18 November was a shattering blow from which he did not recover. Four days later he sent the Queen a detailed account of Lady Canning's final hours as 'The kindness of Your Majesty to Lady Canning has been so invariable and so great that he feels it to be right that your Majesty should receive a sure account of her last illness with as little delay as possible'(VS, pp. 293-4). A large watercolour of Lady Canning's tomb, in the gardens of Government House, Barrackpore, near Calcutta, was painted for the Queen in 1869 by Sir Michael Biddulph and, during the Queen's lifetime, hung at Osborne House, in the Lady in Waiting's bedroom (RL 20258).

Temple of Dendera
Ink with brown and grey wash and white heightening.
34.8 x 25 cm
Dated and inscribed on mount *Dendera / Dec.25. 1855.*

Dendera, one of the finest surviving Egyptian temples, stands forty miles downstream from Luxor and was built in the first century BC Lady Canning described how when she visited it on Christmas Day, 'the inner chambers of the temple were quite dark, and we crept through a hole into a secret passage with very perfect sculpture, and were busy examining them till literally driven out by a cloud of bats' (A. Hare, *The Story of Two Noble Lives,* (1893), II, pp. 8-9).

The Temples of Philae
Watercolour and bodycolour. 21 x 33.2 cm
Dated and inscribed on the mount *Philae. / Dec. 30. 1855*

Philae was the smallest of three islands just above the First Cataract. The temple of Isis was later moved 150 metres north to avoid constant flooding caused by the Aswan dam.

Visited by the Cannings on their journey out to India. Described by Lady Canning in a letter to Queen Victoria as 'that lovely island of Temples & Palm trees, above the first cataract' (Royal Archives, 24 February 1856).

The Governor's Villa, Parell, Bombay
Sepia ink, watercolour, and white heightening.
26.5 x 37.8 cm
Dated and inscribed *Parell. Bombay./ (Governor's Villa) / Feb. 4. 1856*

Lady Canning wrote in her diary for 29 January 1856 that: 'The Governor's house is called Parell, and is five miles off, in a sort of park and large garden, and here it is we are living. I am quite charmed with it... Everything is arranged for coolness, and it seems to answer, for I never felt a pleasanter atmosphere. There are doors in all directions, made like Venetian blinds, and broad verandahs all round the rooms'. This painting is the first mounted under the title 'India' in Lady Canning's album of Indian watercolours, and presumably sent home by her to England.

Cloves, Nutmeg, Tea, Coffee and Mace
Watercolour. 46.3 x 32.8 cm
Inscribed *CLOVES / NUTMEG* and *MACE / COFFEE TEA /* and in pencil *From a Spice Garden / of Mr Thomas – the collector./ Coonoor Ghât. / 1000 ft above the plains* in pencil *from Mr Thomas's Garden / in the fort of Coonoor Ghât.*

From January 1857 with the advent of cooler weather Lady Canning began to make her important series of drawings of rare flowers and trees which she sent home to avoid damage by damp (VS, pp. 225-6). In a letter to her mother she recommended that her sister's work in watercolour should be 'slight & free & yet rich in colour' – advice that she followed herself. In May 1857 the Mutiny broke out and Lord Curzon was later to write of 'the gentle and tragic figure of his accomplished wife' at her husband's side, 'her youth and beauty ebbing away under the appalling strain, her happiness, though not her devotion, shadowed by a cloud, the blame for which had been exclusively his' (VS, p.231). This is mounted in *British and Indian Flowers,* vol. 3, p.76.

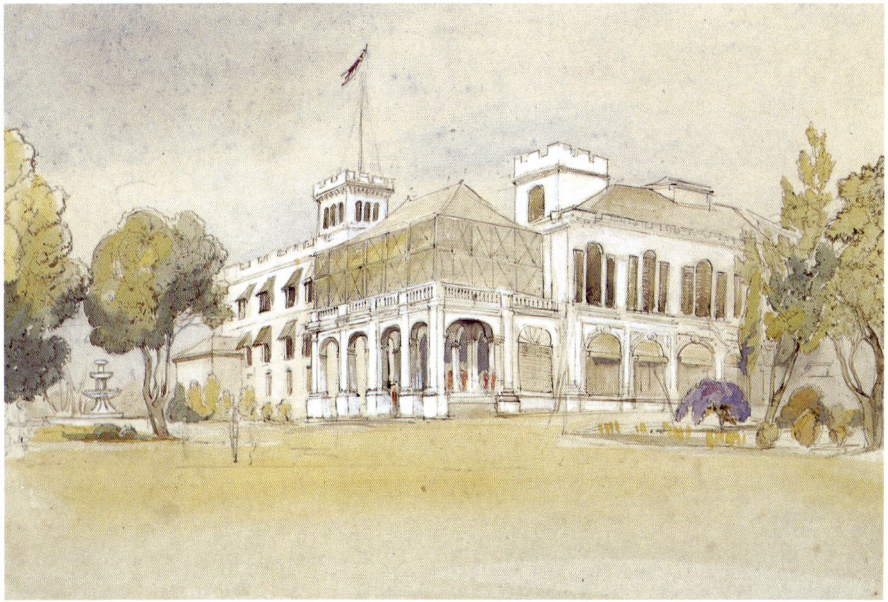

The Governor's Villa, Parell, Bombay.

Louisa, Marchioness of Waterford (1818-1891)

Two volumes bound in dark green leather, with the initials LS on the covers, are with Lady Canning's watercolours in the Library at Harewood House. They contain watercolours and pencil and ink studies by Louisa Stuart, made before and after her marriage. Some are datable from 1839. She married in 1842 and subsequently lived mainly at Curraghmore until the death of her husband in a hunting accident in 1859. Thereafter she lived at Ford Castle in Northumberland, but spent the summer with her mother at Highcliffe Castle in Hampshire. Lady Waterford spent her time doing good work and caring for the poor, but her relaxation was to paint. The large religious scenes with which she covered the walls of the village schoolhouse at Ford between 1862 and 1883 are her major achievement.

'Give us each day our daily bread'
Watercolour, bodycolour and gum arabic. 25.4 x 17.4 cm
Signed and dated *L W / Dec. 5. 1856.* and inscribed on the mount with title as above.

A lady stands at a table distributing slices of bread to children who enter the house on the right.

Documents

by Ann Sumner and Sally Wilks

Lady Canning's Journal for 1840-41
Small parchment volume. 17.7 x 23.2 cm
HAR/Lady Canning 1.1

After her marriage in 1835 Lady Canning travelled extensively with her husband. At the beginning of this journal there is an index of dates and places visited from Gibraltar to Barcelona, Naples and Rome. By July she is back at her father's house Highcliffe, where she was visited by the Clanricardes. The Journal is open on a page where she records going to the railway station with the Clanricardes. The following day, on Thursday 23 July, they went by fly to Lymington where she boarded their yacht *Gondola* with her father and sailed through the Needles and saw the coloured sands on the Isle of Wight. Later that year the couple visited Palermo, Malta and Constantinople.

Letter from Queen Victoria, Buckingham Palace, May 28 1842
Manuscript letter. 18 x 11.6 cm
HAR/Lady Canning c.1841-61

In this letter the young Queen Victoria offers Lady Canning the position of Lady of the Bedchamber, which she explains has become 'vacant' by the resignation of Lady Dalhousie *(see page 4)*.

Draft reply by Lady Canning to Queen Victoria's proposal, not dated.
Manuscript letter. 22.8 x 16.6 cm
HAR/ Lady Canning 4 c.1841-1861

In this draft reply, written by her husband, Lady Canning thanks Queen Victoria for her 'gracious letter' and she accepts the position of serving 'Your Majesty's Royal Person' with 'pride and gratification'.

Letter from Queen Victoria, Windsor Castle, 13 July 1851
Manuscript letter. 17.8 x 11.1 cm
HAR/ Lady Canning 4 c.1841-61

In this letter Queen Victoria acknowledges receipt of a letter from Lady Canning. The Queen reveals how disappointed she is that Lady Canning's sister, Louisa, Lady Waterford has rejected the Queen's offer of becoming one of her Ladies. The reason she declines the offer is because of 'her duties as a wife'. The Queen goes on to stress that the rejection is to be kept 'strictly confidential'.

Lady Canning's Journal for 1850-52
Green leather notebook. 15.8 x 21.2 cm
HAR/Lady Canning 1.6

This Journal is open on a page dating from July 1852, at a time when Lady Canning was on duty on the Isle of Wight. She arrived at Osborne on Saturday 3 July and left on Tuesday 6 July and went to Cowes *(see page 13)*. She describes sitting at a bow window overlooking the River Medina, doing some shopping and then taking a shore boat to visit the Duke of Rutland on the 'Resolution'.